Famille Vve Paris née Laveau

The Tomb of Marie Laveau

in St. Louis Cemetery No. 1

Carolyn Morrow Long

LEFTHANDPRESS

A division of Black Moon Publishing, LLC
New Orleans, Louisiana USA

ISBN: 978-0692766866

United States • United Kingdom • Europe • Australia • India

CONTENTS

Introduction 5

Famille Vve Paris née Laveau
The Tomb of Marie Laveau in St. Louis Cemetery No. 1 6

Who was Marie Laveau? 8
    Personal Life 8
    Voudou 9
    Offerings and Xs 13
    Vandalism 16

The Research Project 19
    Construction and Ownership of the Widow Paris Tomb ... 19
    Successive Multiple Interments 22
    Funeral Records 23
    Burial Books 23

The Widow Paris Tomb 28
    Family 28
    Marie Laveau and Christophe Glapion 29
    The Laveau-Glapion Children 33
    The Glapion-Crocker Descendants 34

The Glapion-Legendre Descendants 39

The Darcantel-Gondron-Eastin Descendants 44

Slaves 45

Friends 45

    Monette 45

    Adams 46

    Llado 49

Neighbors 49

Rentals 50

The Laveau-Glapion Family
and the Widow Paris Tomb After 1897 52

Analysis 57

Who Owns the Widow Paris Tomb? 60

Conclusion 62

Notes 64

Appendix

    Widow Paris tomb 1834-1957 84

    St. Louis tomb 1863-1886 110

    Vault Basin Street Wall 1865-1910 114

INTRODUCTION

Earlier versions of this text were published online by the Louisiana Endowment for the Humanities at *www.knowlouisiana. org/40870/*, and in *New Orleans Genesis*, the quarterly journal of the Genealogical Research Society of New Orleans, Vol. LIV, No. 215, July 2016.

The Sacramental Registers and Burial Books of the Roman Catholic Archdiocese of New Orleans are available to registered researchers at the Office of Archives and Records, 7887 Walmsley Avenue, New Orleans, Dr. Emilie Leumas, archivist. Website: *archives.arch-no. org/*. I am grateful to Dr. Leumas for providing digital images of the most important entries from the Burial Books. The Burial Books are also available on microfilm at the Louisiana Division of the New Orleans Public Library, but the film is scratched and the quality is very poor.

The Archdiocesan Cemeteries Office is located at 1000 Howard Avenue, New Orleans, Sherri Peppo, director. Website: *nolacatholiccemeteries.org/*. The St. Louis Cemeteries Office is located in a small building just inside the gates of St. Louis Cemetery No. 3, 3421 Esplanade Avenue, New Orleans, Alana Mendoza, office manager. The archival holdings of the main Cemeteries Office and the St. Louis Cemeteries Office are not available to researchers.

The Dead Space project for St. Louis Cemetery No. 1 was carried out in 2002-2003 by the Historic Preservation Program, Graduate School of Fine Arts, University of Pennsylvania, Frank Matero, director. Website: *www.noladeadspace.com/*; cemetery map: *www.noladeadspace.com/st-louis-no-1-map*. Most useful is the tomb inventory and database at *www.noladeadspace.com/pdfs/ Inventory%20KeyData.pdf*, which includes a photograph of each tomb and can be searched by name or location.

Carolyn Morrow Long is an artist and writer, author of *Spiritual Merchants: Religion, Magic, and Commerce* (University of Tennessee Press 2001), *A New Orleans Voudou Priestess: The Legend and Reality of Marie Laveau* (University Press of Florida 2006), and *Madame Lalaurie, Mistress of the Haunted House* (University Press of Florida 2012).

THE TOMB OF MARIE LAVEAU IN ST. LOUIS CEMETERY NO. 1

S t. Louis Cemetery No. 1 lies just outside the Vieux Carré (French Quarter), in the square bounded by Basin, Conti, Tremé, and St. Louis streets. This sacred place was established during the Spanish colonial period in 1789 to replace an even earlier graveyard on St. Peter Street between Rampart and Burgundy. St. Louis Cemetery No. 1 is noted for its above-ground tombs situated along winding *allées,* or aisles. There are free-standing family tombs with several vaults, grand multi-vaulted "society tombs," and three tiers, or "ranges," of vaults in the massive walls, nine feet thick and twelve feet high, that enclose the cemetery on all sides. Owing to the practice of multiple interments, these burial sites have come to house an astonishing number of bodies. The tombs and walls are constructed of soft, locally made brick and mortar covered by lime-based stucco and coated with a lime-based wash.[1] St. Louis Cemetery No. 1, like all of New Orleans' Catholic cemeteries, is owned by the Archdiocese of New Orleans and is administered by the Archdiocesan Cemeteries Office.

A few steps from the cemetery's Basin Street gate stands the resting place of New Orleans' most celebrated Voudou priestess, Marie Laveau. The pedimented three-vault tomb bears the inscription *Famille Vᵛᴱ Paris née Laveau* (Family of the Widow Paris born Laveau). As part of a self-guided tour conceived by the Archdiocese in 1962, a bronze plaque was affixed to the front, stating that: "This Greek revival tomb is reputed burial place of the notorious 'voodoo queen.' A mystic cult, voodooism, of African origin, was brought to New Orleans from Santo Domingo [Haiti] and flourished in the 19th century. Marie Laveau was the most widely known of many practitioners of the cult."[2]

fig. 1: Wall vaults and free-standing tombs in St. Louis Cemetery No. 1. Photo by Carolyn Long, 1987.

fig. 2: Tomb of the Widow Paris née Laveau. Photo by Carolyn Long, 2014.

Who was Marie Laveau?

Personal Life

The nineteenth century Voudou priestess Marie Laveau is indeed one of New Orleans' most iconic figures. Now viewed as a near-fictional character, it is easy to forget that she was a real person, a free woman of color descended from enslaved Africans and French colonists.

Marie's great-grandmother, called Marguerite, was probably born in Senegal and sold into slavery as a child. She is likely to have been a Wolof, a people noted for their trading and marketing skills and considered to be extraordinarily intelligent and handsome. In 1756, twenty-year-old Marguerite and her daughter Catherine, age two, were listed in the property inventory of the white Creole Henry Roche *dit* (known as) Belaire, a master shoemaker and a man of some wealth. Catherine's father was a black man called Jean Belaire about whom nothing further is known.

Catherine grew up in the household of Henry Roche. He may have fathered her mixed-race children, one of whom, Marguerite, became the mother of Marie Laveau. After enduring two more owners, in 1784 Catherine became the property of the free woman of color Françoise Pomet. In 1795, at the age of forty-two, Catherine paid the formidable sum of $600 cash to Pomet and thereby became a free person. She subsequently took Henry as her surname, established herself as a successful market woman, bought land, and commissioned the construction of a cottage on St. Ann Street between Rampart and Burgundy.

Catherine's daughter, Marguerite Henry, was freed by her owner in 1890. She had several children with the Frenchman Henri Darcantel, but her famous daughter Marie Laveau resulted from a brief relationship with Charles Laveaux, a prosperous free-colored businessman. Marie was born on September 10, 1801, and was baptized at St. Louis Cathedral with her grandmother Catherine standing as godmother. She was probably raised in Catherine's home at 152 (now 1020-1022) St. Ann Street.

In 1819, Marie was married at St. Louis Cathedral to Jacques Paris, a free man of color from Saint-Domingue (now Haiti). Paris died or disappeared around 1824, and his death and interment records have never been discovered. Marie was henceforth designated in official documents as the Widow Paris.

She later entered into a life partnership with Louis Christophe Dominique Duminy de Glapion, a white man of noble French ancestry. The couple could not marry legally because of Louisiana's anti-miscegenation law, but Marie sometimes went by the name Marie Glapion or Madame Christophe Glapion. Marie and Christophe had seven children together between 1827 and 1838: Marie Eloise (or Helöise) Euchariste, Marie Louise Caroline, Christophe, Jean Baptiste, François, Marie Philomène, and Archange. Only Eloise Euchariste and Philomène survived to adulthood. When Marie's grandmother Catherine Henry died, Christophe Glapion bought the cottage on St. Ann Street and it remained the Laveau-Glapion family home for nearly a hundred years.

Marie was renowned for her acts of charity and community service. She provided food and housing to the poor, nursed yellow fever and cholera victims during the city's frequent epidemics, sponsored the education of an orphaned boy at the Catholic Institution for Indigent Orphans, and posted bond for free women of color accused of minor crimes. She visited condemned prisoners, built altars in their cells, and prayed with them in their final hours. As we will see, she also offered the use of her tomb to strangers who had no burial place of their own.[3] Her life and works embody what are known in the Catholic Church as the Corporal Works of Mercy, in which the faithful are instructed to "feed the hungry, give drink to the thirsty, clothe the naked, shelter the homeless, visit the sick, visit the imprisoned, and bury the dead."

VOUDOU

Marie Laveau was a devout Catholic and a lifelong member of St. Louis Cathedral, where she was baptized and married and attended mass regularly. She ensured that all her children were baptized there and stood as godmother at the baptisms of her nephew and granddaughter. Her funeral was conducted by a priest of the Cathedral. She also retained the religion of her African ancestors, and by the 1830s she had assumed leadership of a multiracial, mostly female Voudou congregation. By all accounts, in addition to her genuine spiritual gifts, Marie possessed extraordinary beauty, a magnetic personality, and a flair for showmanship. Even during her lifetime she had become a cult figure. She developed a following among enslaved and free people of color as well as upper-class white New Orleanians and visitors to the city, who were welcome at her ceremonies and numbered among her clients.

New Orleans Voudou is the only indigenous North American example of the New World Afro-Catholic religions common to the Caribbean and South America. When enslaved Africans were exposed to Catholicism, they found many elements to which they could relate. The supreme being common to most West African belief systems was analogous to God the Father, and the African deities and ancestors who serve as intermediaries between men and the supreme being became identified with the Virgin Mary and the other saints. The rituals, music, vestments and miracle-working objects of the Catholic Church seemed intrinsically familiar to Africans whose religious ceremonies stressed chanting, drumming, dance, elaborate costumes, and the use of spirit-embodying amulets. Through a process of creative borrowing and adaptation, they reinterpreted Catholicism to suit their own needs, resulting in the evolution of Haitian Vodou, Cuban Santería, Brazilian Candomblé, and New Orleans Voudou. The guiding principal of these African-influenced religions was balance between the individual, the community, the natural environment, and the deities.

In the early years of the nineteenth century, there were still some Africans among New Orleans' slaves and free blacks. In addition, many enslaved and free Africans had arrived in New Orleans from Haiti at the turn of the nineteenth century. These African-born community elders preserved elements of their traditional religions, in which women took responsibility for initiating their daughters. Marie Laveau's great-grandmother, grandmother, and mother could have served the Voudou spirits in addition to God the Father, Jesus, and the saints of the Catholic Church. Any or all of these neighbors and kinswomen might have trained the young Marie in the religion

10

of her ancestors. She would have perceived Catholicism and Voudou as different, but not conflicting, ways of serving the spiritual forces that govern the world.

Descriptions of the Voudou ceremonies and practices of Marie Laveau and her contemporaries are found in interviews conducted by the Louisiana Writers' Project, a program created by the federal government during the Great Depression under the auspices of the Works Projects Administration. Writers' Project fieldworkers sought out black New Orleanians born in the 1860s and '70s who had grown up in Marie Laveau's neighborhood, were friends with her family, or had been members of her congregation. According to these interviews, Marie's front room had multiple altars laden with candles, images of the saints, flowers, and other offerings. Here she presided over weekly Friday night meetings, at which participants were dressed in white. Herbs, cooked foods, liquor, candles, and coins were arranged on a white cloth on the ground or the floor, in accordance with a custom referred to as "spreading a feast for the spirits." The service began with Catholic prayers, such as the Hail Mary and the Our Father. Marie would pour out libations of water or wine, salute the four cardinal directions, and rap three times on the

fig. 3: Illustration for George Washington Cable's "Creole Slave Songs," *Century Magazine,* 1886, collection of Carolyn Long. This drawing depicts a Voudou ceremony, possibly at Marie Laveau's cottage. Musicians play African-style instruments, and the congregation sings and dances around the "feast spread for the spirits" placed on a white cloth.

ground "in the name of the Father, Son, and Holy Ghost." Afterwards the participants would chant and dance. All of these rituals were intended to call the spirits to enter the bodies of the faithful and provide counsel to the congregation. A shared meal followed the religious portion of the service.[4]

In addition to holding regular services for her followers, Marie Laveau also gave consultations and performed ceremonies for individual clients. Louisiana Writers' Project interviewees told of rituals to attract and control a lover, bring about a marriage, improve business, and win in court, as well as those for negative purposes. Marie served the local community of color, but also, according to the 1881 obituary published in the *New York Times,* she received "Louisiana's greatest men and most distinguished visitors...lawyers, legislators, planters, and merchants, [who] all came to pay their respects and seek her offices."[5]

The most important of the Voudou ceremonies took place on the shore of Lake Pontchartrain on June 23, the Eve of St. John the Baptist. St. John's Eve is two days after the summer solstice. In pre-Christian Europe the summer solstice was believed to be a time when the human world and the spirit world intersect, and people observed this time of heightened consciousness by lighting bonfires and immersing themselves in sacred bodies of water. The Feast of St. John was grafted onto this pagan ritual. The celebration of St. John's Eve was introduced into Louisiana by French and Spanish colonists, and at some undetermined time it was adopted by people of African descent. According to newspaper articles and the Louisiana Writers' Project interviews, Marie Laveau led this celebration from sometime in the 1830s until the early 1870s. These accounts vary considerably, but all describe bonfires, drumming, singing, dancing, ritual bathing, and a communal feast.[6]

Following the immense social and economic changes brought about by the Civil War, emancipation of the slaves, and the attempted (and ultimately failed) reforms of Reconstruction, local newspapers became increasingly racist and hostile to any sort of African-based practice. An 1869 article in the *New Orleans Commercial Bulletin* observed derisively that "June is the time devoted by the Voudou worshipers to...their most sacred and therefore most revolting rites. Midnight dances, bathing and eating, together with other less innocent pleasures, make the early summer a time of unrestrained orgies for the blacks." The *Commercial Bulletin* announced that the summer of 1869 was "marked by the coronation of a new Voudou queen in the place of the celebrated Marie Laveau, who has held her office for a quarter of a century and is now superannuated in her seventieth year." (Marie was actually a few months short of her sixty-seventh birthday.) Taking a poke at the newly freed slaves, the *Commercial Bulletin* reporter quipped that now "a more youthful hand puts up love philters and makes fetishes for the intelligent freedmen, who elect governors and members of Congress out of their own number."[7] Every summer New Orleans journalists trekked out to Lake Pontchartrain on St. John's Eve, always hoping to see Marie Laveau, and almost always disappointed. In 1870 Marie was said to have been present at the St. John's Eve celebration. In 1872 a reporter identified the officiating priestess as Marie Laveau.[8] After that there were no further accounts of public appearances by the "Voudou Queen," but the St. John's Eve stories continued, and became increasingly sensationalistic, through the 1890s.

As Marie gradually became incapacitated by old age, she retired to her cottage on St. Ann Street and was cared for by her daughter Philomène. She died at home on June 15, 1881. Following a funeral conducted the next day by a priest of St. Louis Cathedral, she was interred in her family tomb in St. Louis Cemetery No. 1 bearing the inscription *Famille Vve Paris née Laveau.*

OFFERINGS AND XS

At some time, perhaps shortly after Marie Laveau died in 1881, followers began to solicit contact with her spirit by leaving offerings and drawing the sign of the cross on her tomb. These practices are rooted in both European and African religious traditions. There is a universal human impulse to offer gifts of flowers and things that the dead would have enjoyed, placing these memorial tributes not only on the burial places of family members but also the graves of public figures who are considered artistically or spiritually powerful. Regarding the cross marks, the Christian symbolism is obvious, and in African religious tradition two crossed lines represent the intersection of the human and spirit worlds.[9] These rituals were certainly in use by the early twentieth century, when newspaper

fig. 4: Widow Paris tomb with offerings and Xs. Photo by Carolyn Long, 2013.

articles referred to the offerings and cross marks at the Widow Paris tomb and at a wall vault in St. Louis Cemetery No. 2 that is also associated with Voudou. In 1921 an article in the *New Orleans Times-Picayune* described the "negroes" and "nice looking young [white] ladies" who "with a piece of shell from the walk" would "make a cross on the bricks [of the] strange old Wishing Vault in St. Louis Cemetery No. 2" and "repeat their wish out loud." In 1928 the *New Orleans Morning Tribune* reported that on All Saints' Day large crowds "came to seek the favor of Marie Laveau...marked a cross upon her tomb, and made a wish." In 1934 the *Times-Picayune* carried an article about Marie Laveau, noting that "even at the present time...her followers...scratch little crosses on the...front of her tomb." A 1938 *Times-Picayune* article conceded that the "Voodoo Queen" is buried in St. Louis Cemetery No. 1, but that "one of the queer old oven vaults" in St. Louis Cemetery No. 2 had become a focus of the Voudou community: "A cross mark on the door as a wish is made and a coin slipped behind the loose brick will work a certain charm."[10]

In 1940 workers for the Louisiana Writers' Project learned, in an interview with the sexton of St. Louis Cemetery No. 1, that "Negroes and whites come almost daily to leave offerings to Marie's spirit [at the Widow Paris tomb]. They make crosses with red brick, charcoal, and sharp rocks which [the sexton], acting under orders of the priests of St. Louis Cathedral, immediately removes." The Writers' Project report noted that "close observation discloses scratched crosses under the fresh whitewash."[11] These printed and oral accounts always refer to "crosses" or "cross marks," not Xs.

The Widow Paris tomb became a major tourist attraction in the later twentieth century, and at some point the crosses morphed into Xs. For years the tomb was easily recognizable by the offerings of flowers, fruit, candies, coins, liquor, candles, and Mardi Gras beads placed on the pavement before it, and the X marks covering the walls and marble inscription tablets.

The Xs have been a particularly contentious issue. As we learn from the Louisiana Writers' Project interview, even in 1940 the Archdiocese objected to Laveau devotees marking crosses on the Widow Paris tomb. By the late 1990s preservationists and the Archdiocesan Cemeteries Office were condemning the practice as "desecration" or "graffiti," and arguing that it was introduced by unscrupulous tour guides in the 1960s and has no basis in Voudou tradition. The offerings were referred to as "litter" and, according to the Cemeteries Office, "are not considered sacred in Catholic cemeteries."

In 1978 I spent two weeks in New Orleans and, like so many others, fell in love with the city and recognized it as my spiritual home. Early one morning I went alone to St. Louis Cemetery No. 1 and was immediately captivated by the Marie Laveau/Widow Paris tomb.

An elderly gentleman who was apparently a cemetery caretaker—he was not a paid tour guide—instructed me to leave a little offering for Marie, place my hand on the tomb, say a prayer to her spirit, take a bit of soft red brick from a crumbling tomb nearby, and draw an X mark. At the time, I failed to realize that even this seemingly benign practice contributed to the deterioration of adjacent tombs from which brick fragments were being removed.

Later on, thoughtless visitors, with no understanding of the Voudou religion and no awareness of the value and fragility of New Orleans' historic cemeteries, began to draw not one but three Xs with red paint, permanent markers, lipstick, and fingernail polish. Use of these synthetic oil-and-chemical-based materials damaged the stuccoed front and sides of the tomb and especially the marble tablets, penetrating the surface and rendering the inscriptions illegible. In 2005 the city of New Orleans passed an ordinance outlawing the marking of tombs or otherwise defacing cemetery property, with fines from $500 to $10,000 and from six months to ten years in jail. A warning sign is now posted by the front gate.[12]

VANDALISM

In mid-December 2013, somebody scaled the cemetery wall during the night, painted the Widow Paris tomb with bright "Pepto Bismol" pink latex paint, and applied a coating of white latex to the marble inscription tablets. (see photograph on back cover) An out-of-town devotee, making her annual visit to honor Marie Laveau, reported the shocking discovery to a cemetery custodian. The Archdiocesan Cemeteries Office dispatched workmen to remove the latex paint by pressure washing. This extreme treatment indeed got rid of the paint, but it also dislodged layers of stucco and lime wash, exposing the soft brick underneath. Save Our Cemeteries, a non-profit cemetery preservation group, eventually came to an agreement with the Cemeteries Office to raise funds and have the tomb completely restored by experts from Bayou Preservation LLC. The work entailed rebuilding the roof, renewing the stucco on the walls followed by several coats of lime wash, and cleaning the marble tablets. The restoration was finished in time for All Saints' Day 2014.[13] Nobody was ever arrested for painting the tomb, but those in the

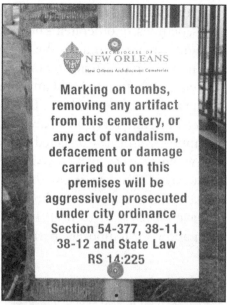

fig. 5: Sign at the Basin Street gate to St. Louis Cemetery No. 1 prohibiting marking on tombs. Photo by Carolyn Long, 2015.

know believe that the perpetrator was a "mentally disturbed homeless kid" who thought he was performing a service by obliterating the X marks.

Unlawful entry and vandalism at St. Louis Cemetery No. 1 continued after the incident of the pink paint. A young man boasted on Facebook that he and his girlfriend had gone over the wall at night, pitched a tent, and lived in the back of the cemetery for months. In April 2014, the *New Orleans Times-Picayune* reported on a pair of renegade tour guides who removed bricks from the sides of tombs, allowing tourists to insert their cameras or reach inside to snatch a souvenir bone.[14] In January 2015, vandals broke into the Barbarin Family Musicians' Tomb and pulled bones out onto the sidewalk.

The Archdiocese had finally had enough, announcing that effective March 1, 2015, nobody would be admitted to St. Louis Cemetery No. 1 unless accompanied by a licensed and insured tour guide registered with the Archdiocesan Cemeteries Office. Tour companies were charged a hefty annual sum for a permit covering all their employees. The Cemeteries Office stated that fees would "go toward staffing the cemetery during the day, beefing up security at night, and help with overall restoration." Tour company owners signed an agreement not to allow group participants to "vandalize and/or deface any tomb" by "placing candles, beans, pennies, or other items near or on any tombs, and/or marking any tombs in any manner." The agreement went on to ban tour guides from allowing participants to bring in "any food or beverages" and to "ensure that no trash of any kind is left on the premises..."[15] An article about the new rules in the online edition of the *New Orleans Times-Picayune* received many comments. While some readers were supportive, others objected to being forced to pay for a guided tour when unaccompanied visitors had previously entered the cemetery for free.[16] To their credit, the Cemeteries Office has since issued permanent passes to those who can document that they own tombs or have family buried in St. Louis Cemetery No. 1, and researchers can apply for temporary permission to enter the cemetery.

Ashes to dust **TOUR GUIDES ACCUSED OF DESECRATING CEMETERY**

The crumbling historic St. Louis No. 1 is further threatened by unlicensed guides

Bricks have been removed from a tomb in St. Louis Cemetery No. 1, exposing an iron casket.

MAIA SETTLE

By Richard A. Webster
Staff writer

Buggy driver Maia Settle knew there was a problem Monday when a customer told her there was a tour guide inside St. Louis Cemetery No. 1 reaching into tombs and pulling out jawbones to show the crowds.

Settle said she knew of one man, named Walter, who for years had been giving unlicensed tours of the cemetery. He typically removed one brick from the tombs, creating a hole large enough to reach inside. He would hold a camera taken from one of the tourists, snap several pictures, return the camera and put the brick back in place.

The photos of exposed femurs or ancient coffins were apparently meant to be souvenirs of their trip to New Orleans, she said.

See **CEMETERIES**, *A-10*

Archdiocese says it is increasing security measures at cemeteries

CEMETERIES, *from A-1*

But Walter was not known to remove body parts.

Settle said she wanted to investigate the matter further. So she spent her day off walking through St. Louis No. 1 taking photos.

She found one tomb with a hole large enough to see the cast iron casket inside. Someone had dragged the coffin closer to the opening to provide a better view.

This, apparently, was not the work of Walter but someone new. The desecration of such a personal and historic place was too much for Settle to take.

"Everybody I know from New Orleans is highly offended," said Settle, who sent her pictures to the Archdiocese of New Orleans, which owns the cemetery, and Taxicab Bureau Director Malachi Hull, who oversees tour-guide licensing.

"As Catholics, people are offended. As tour guides, people are offended. My family goes back here to 1718. When these people start breaking up the tombs and destroying the last piece of history we have, that's when we know we need to do something."

The New Orleans Police Department arrested Walter Ross, 53, on Tuesday on charges of desecration of graves and criminal trespass. Police

wall and held a wedding ceremony in St. Louis No. 1, she said.

The most infamous example of vandalism occurred in December when someone painted the tomb of Voodoo queen Marie Laveau pink.

However, breaking into a tomb and either removing someone's remains or taking pictures of them is far more serious, Stevenson said.

"It's not King Tut in that tomb; it's somebody's dead grandmother," he said. "And they deserve more respect than being treated like a sideshow freak."

'The bones mingle together'

In most of the tombs, the remains have long since turned to dust, Green said there are up to eight burials each year at St. Louis No. 1.

Traditionally, a body was inserted into a wooden coffin into the tomb, where it was left for a year and one day, when the tomb was reopened. Whatever was left inside after sitting in 300-degree heat for a year — typically bones and the coffin padding and handles — was swept into the pit at the bottom of the tomb, called a caveau.

"All the bones mingle together. We call it the ultimate in family togetherness," Green said.

Since contemporary people are taller and wider than their Creole ancestory, many of their coffins can't fit into the tombs.

are doing is akin to throwing a brick through stained glass window at a cathedral," Stevenson said. "The people who built our city and culture are buried in there. Regardless of someone's religious background, respect

PHOTOS BY MAIA SETTLE

Unlicensed tour guides are removing bricks from tombs in St. Louis Cemetery No. 1 so that tourists can take a look at the remains inside, cemetery advocates say. This creates gaping holes in the tombs, exposing the remains inside to theft. Vandalism and theft have long been problems at New Orleans' cemeteries.

fig. 6: Article on vandalism at St. Louis Cemetery No. 1 from the *New Orleans Times-Picayune*, April 27, 2014.

THE RESEARCH PROJECT

P ublicity over the pink paint episode and other acts of vandalism, plus the new restrictions on cemetery access, focused public interest in the Widow Paris tomb and generated inquiries about who exactly is buried there. Some even questioned whether Marie Laveau herself actually rests in this tomb. To address these issues, I turned to the rich archival resources available for Orleans Parish. Most important were the records at the Office of Archives and Records of the Archdiocese of New Orleans. I also used the "Dead Space" survey of St. Louis Cemetery No. 1, conducted in 2001-2002 by the University of Pennsylvania School of Fine Arts graduate program in historic preservation. The Dead Space team, as part of their effort, created a searchable online map and database for every tomb in the cemetery. These key sources were supplemented by the U.S. census; civil birth, marriage, and death certificates; city directories; newspaper articles; and the Robinson's Atlas and Sanborn Fire Insurance Maps for the City of New Orleans.

CONSTRUCTION AND OWNERSHIP
OF THE WIDOW PARIS TOMB

Although St. Louis Cemetery No. 1 belongs to and is administered by the Archdiocese, individual tombs are the private property of the families who hold the official "title of ownership."[17] In the early years of St. Louis Cemetery No. 1, a family desiring a place of interment for their dead would buy a lot from the wardens of St. Louis Cathedral and engage a builder to erect a tomb. One of my objectives in undertaking this research was to learn when the Widow Paris tomb was constructed and by whom it was commissioned. Did Marie Laveau order it built to receive the remains of her loved ones, did she buy it from the original owner, or, as one legend asserts, was it donated to her by an admirer? Neither the Archdiocesan Archives nor the Archdiocesan Cemeteries Office had any record of the construction date or original ownership of the tomb.

The Cemeteries Office provided a digital image of a ledger book page indicating that on December 16, 1925, a duplicate title of ownership for the Widow Paris tomb, specified as "lot 9, 2nd alley left Conti to St. Louis" was issued in the name of Archange Glapion by the Reverend Albert Antoine, rector of St. Louis Cathedral. I was also given a photocopy of an ownership card describing the tomb as "No. 7 (9 on title), alley No. 2 left facing St. Louis Street, Archange Glapion owner."[18] Archange was the youngest child of Marie Laveau and Christophe Glapion; he died in 1845 at the age of seven years, seven months. Why this little boy was designated in 1925 as the legal owner of the tomb remains a mystery.

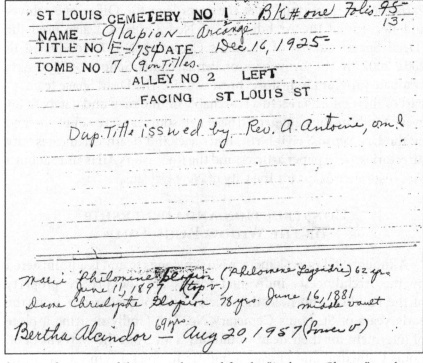

fig. 7: A photocopy of the ownership card for the "Archange Glapion" tomb was provided by Alana Mendoza, superintendent of the St. Louis Cemeteries Office.

An interesting discovery was made by Bayou Preservation LLC during the course of their restoration work. Removal of the stucco damaged by pressure washing revealed that the lower and middle vaults were built with older, harder, tan bricks, and the upper vault was built of softer red bricks, indicating that it was added later.[19] This does not, however, provide an exact construction date for either level of the tomb.

fig. 8: Photo showing the older layer of bricks on the lower level contrasted with the newer layer of bricks on the upper level. Photo courtesy of Bayou Preservation LLC.

The Widow Paris tomb, or at least the lower and middle vaults, was probably in place by 1831 when Marie's grandmother, Catherine Henry, died. We are fortunate to have a receipt for Catherine's funeral from *la fabrique de l'Eglise St. Louis de la Nouvelle Orleans pour frais de l'Enterrenent de feue Catherine Henry inhumée le 19 Juin 1831* (the wardens of the Church of St. Louis of New Orleans for costs of the Interment of the late Catherine Henry buried June 19, 1831). This document, which was attached to Catherine's succession papers, listed payment for *assistances de 2 prêtres, 2 chantres, 3 infants de choeur, 1 suisse, and droits et bénéfice de la fabrique* (two priests, two cantors, three choir boys, one usher, and a fee for "rights and benefits" of the church wardens) totaling $29.50. The printed receipt form includes lines for *emplacement pour bâtir une tombe* (location to build a tomb) and *tombe vendue par la fabrique* (tomb sold by the wardens). No charges were written in for these items, indicating that the family already owned a cemetery plot and tomb.[20]

SUCCESSIVE MULTIPLE INTERMENTS

Eighty-four people were laid to rest in the Widow Paris tomb. Readers unfamiliar with New Orleans cemetery customs may be surprised by the practice of successive multiple interments in the same tomb, and even in the same vault. Unembalmed bodies were placed in simple wooden coffins, and the funeral and entombment took place within a day of death. The Archdiocesan Cemeteries Office has decreed that a vault cannot be opened to receive another body until the passage of "a year and a day." After this, the remains are assumed to have crumbled to dust. Dr. Bennet Dowler, writing in the *Medical and Surgical Journal* of November 1850, declared that "the body is completely decomposed, the bones separated, and offensive gases dissipated in about three months in the hot season and in six months in winter."[21]

fig. 9: The Fontana family tomb in St. Louis Cemetery No. 1 is an example of a tomb with an elevated base and a protruding shelf below the lower vault, indicating that it has a receiving vault. Photo by Carolyn Long, 2015.

When the vault was needed for the next interment, a cemetery worker temporarily removed the marble tablet and the bricks that seal the opening, raked out and burned the pieces of the wooden coffin, and pushed what remained of the bones to the back. After the new coffin was inserted, the bricks and tablet were replaced. Some tombs have a receiving vault underneath, and the bones would fall down into this chamber through a slot; such tombs can be recognized by an elevated base and a protruding shelf below the lower vault.[22] The Widow Paris tomb does not have such a chamber.

Funeral Records

Because Marie Laveau was an active member of the congregation of St. Louis Cathedral, there is ample documentation of the baptisms, marriages, funerals, and interments of herself and her family. St. Louis Cathedral has funeral records for Marie's mother, Marguerite Henry Darcantel (died 1825); her grandmother, Catherine Henry (died 1831); and for Marie and Christophe's children who died in infancy—Marie Louise Caroline (1829), Christophe (1831), Jean Baptiste (1832), and François (1834). There is no funeral record for Archange, Eloise Euchariste, or Philomène because the Cathedral ceased to maintain a funeral register after 1842. None of the funeral records describes the exact place of interment, but they do state that the body was *inhume dans le Cimetière de cette Paroisse de St. Louis de la Nouvelle Orleans* (buried in the cemetery of this Parish of St. Louis of New Orleans).[23] There is a good possibility that Marie's mother, grandmother, and her other children are interred in the Widow Paris tomb.

Burial Books

The Burial Books were the most valuable source of information. Instead of searching for known relatives of Marie Laveau or friends of her family, I was looking for any person interred in the Widow Paris tomb in St. Louis Cemetery No. 1.

The earliest of the books, roughly covering the years 1833 to 1857, gave the name of the deceased, date of interment, age, race, class of funeral, and sometimes added the notation *cimetière ancien* (old cemetery), meaning St. Louis No. 1; *cimetière nouvelle* (new cemetery, meaning St. Louis No. 2, consecrated in 1823); or *Bayou* (meaning the now-defunct potters' field along Bayou St. John). The books never provide a description or precise location of the tomb in which the deceased was interred. There are gaps in the chronology of these early books. Fortunately, the interments of some family members are known from the names on the marble inscription tablets of the Widow Paris tomb.

The most useful information for this study begins to appear in the Burial Book for December 23, 1859-December 31, 1864, and this series continues, with some variations, through the book for January 1, 1913-December 5, 1919. These wonderful records give the name and sometimes the parents or spouse of the deceased, age, race *(blanc or couleur)*, place of birth, date and cause of death, home address or place of death, name of certifying physician, and date of interment. Most importantly, the entries provide a description and location of the tomb where burial took place. The entries often specified in which of the three vaults the body was placed. The French words *voute, trou, four,* or *caveau* were used interchangeably for vault, with *haut* meaning the top, *milieu* the middle, and *bas* the lower.

It was not unusual for a body to be moved to another tomb or another cemetery; this was always indicated by a notation written perpendicularly across the original Burial Book entry. In the days when wooden coffins were used, the removal would have to be done before, or at the time of, the next interment in that vault. Once the old coffin was discarded and the bone fragments were pushed to the back or dropped down into the receiving vault, it would be impossible to isolate the remains of any particular person. It was much easier to move a body after metal caskets and embalming were introduced in the twentieth century. (See figure 21, pg 47, the interment entry for Lucien Adams Jr., for an example of a notation of removal.)

During Marie Laveau's lifetime and for a few years after her 1881 death, the final line of each entry for the Widow Paris tomb was always some variation on the phrase *Inhumé dans la tombe de Mme Veuve Paris née Marie Laveau seconde allée au droite* (buried in the tomb of Madame Widow Paris born Marie Laveau, second aisle on the right). In the later 1880s and 1890s it was called the "Philomène Glapion tomb." In the early twentieth century, after Philomène had died and most of the family had dispersed, it was called the "Blair

Legendre tomb," referring to Philomène's only surviving son who was overseeing its use. It was never called the "Archange Glapion tomb."

The fifty-nine-year run of highly informative Burial Books ended in 1919. There is no book for 1920, and after that the format became much less useful. The book for August 16, 1921-September 19, 1929, gives only the name of the deceased, cause of death, date, age, doctor, and undertaker; sometimes race is indicated by W(white) or C (colored) noted in the margin. Instead of describing the tomb by family name and location, only the "coordinates" of tomb and alley number are given. The Widow Paris tomb, for example, was simply "No. 7 alley 2-L." A variation of this format continues in the final book of the series, September 22, 1939-February 26, 1973, with name, age, date of death, Board of Health permit number, and name of funeral home; sometimes a family name was added. A "folio number" was also noted, indicating that the information was copied from some other book that is now presumably lost.

A page-by-page search of 140 years of burial records (1833-1973) revealed an amazing eighty-four people who were laid to rest in the three-vault Widow Paris tomb. This includes not only Laveau-Glapion family members but also slaves, friends, neighbors, and total strangers. This study also led to the surprising discovery that Marie Laveau owned a two-vault tomb across the cemetery on the St. Louis Street side, in use between 1863 and 1886, and a vault in the Basin Street wall, in use between 1865 and 1910. Each held the remains of thirteen people.

The two-vault tomb was described in one burial entry as being "on the St. Louis Street alley near the mortar bed," evidently the place where mortar for building the brick tombs was mixed. Others specified it as being near the Guichard and Jarreau tombs.[24] The Guichard and Jarreau tombs appear on the Dead Space online map in the St. Louis aisle surrounded by a paved open space that might have once been the mortar bed. The exact location of this other tomb owned by Marie Laveau cannot be determined.

The Basin Street wall vault is described as "No. 81 bearing the inscription Lucy Henderson (sometimes Lucy Anderson), lower range."[25] Counting from the Basin Street gate, the eighty-first vault is indeed in the lower range. This section of the wall has subsided considerably, so that now only the top of an arched vault is visible; it has no marble tablet and no inscription. This may or may not be the vault owned by Marie Laveau.

The Cemeteries Office turned up no ownership records for either of the sites. None of the deceased who were placed in these alternative spaces had any apparent connection to Marie Laveau and her family. Databases of all burials in the Widow Paris tomb, the tomb on the St. Louis aisle, and the Basin Street wall vault are included in the appendix.

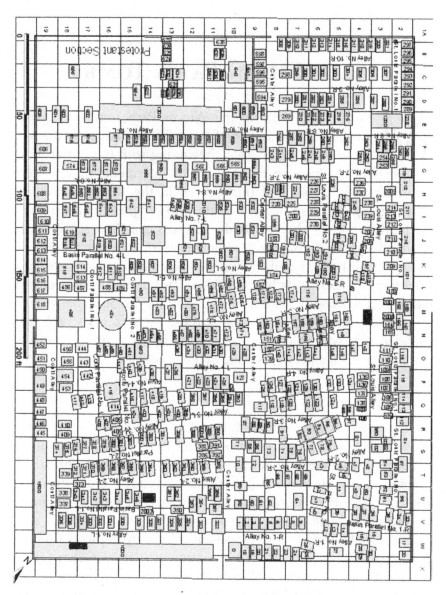

fig. 10: This map of St. Louis Cemetery No. 1 from the Dead Space project shows the location of the Widow Paris tomb (U-14) and the approximate location of the Basin Street wall vault (W-18)) and the two-vault tomb near St. Louis Street (M-5) owned by Marie Laveau. The Basin Street gate is at the bottom, Conti Street on the left and St. Louis Street on the right.www.noladeadspace.com/st-louis-no-1-map.

THE WIDOW PARIS TOMB

Most of the burials in the Widow Paris tomb took place during Marie Laveau's lifetime. There were at least seven between 1834 and 1855. Beginning with the Burial Book for 1859-1864, which specified place of interment, sixteen were recorded in the 1860s and thirty-seven in the 1870s. In the late 1870s the records also began to state who ordered the opening of the tomb to receive the next body; this was usually Marie or, later on, her daughter Philomène Glapion Legendre. Between the time of Marie's death in 1881 and Philomène's passing in 1897, there were twenty more interments in the Widow Paris tomb. There were six interments between 1898 and 1917, and in 1957 one final person was laid to rest there. Not counting those for whom no vault was specified, twenty people were placed in the upper vault, seventeen in the middle vault, and twenty-nine in the lower vault.

FAMILY

Of the eighty-four people interred in the Widow Paris tomb between 1834 and 1957, only twenty-five were verified or assumed to be family members. In addition to Marie Laveau and Christophe Glapion, four of their children, nine grandchildren plus the domestic partner of a grandson, two grandnephews, and six great-grandchildren were laid to rest in the tomb.

In chronological order of interment, they were François Glapion 1834, Archange Glapion 1845, Joseph Eugène Crocker 1845, Esmeralda Crocker 1850, Christophe Duminy de Glapion 1855, Eugène Eastin 1856,Widow Oscar *née* Glapion (possibly Eloise Euchariste Glapion) 1860, Edouard Eastin 1860, Eugènie Legendre 1866, Joseph Legendre 1870, Charles Legendre 1870, Adelai Aldina Crocker 1871, Henry Raphael Glapion 1873, Antoine Raphael Glapion 1874, Manuel Legendre 1876, Onesta Crocker Glapion 1876, Marie Laveau 1881, Victor Pierre Crocker 1892, Antoinette Santenac

1894, Marita Santenac 1894, Ernestine Llado 1897, Clara Westenberg 1897, Marie Legendre 1897, Philomène Glapion Legendre 1897, and Alexandre Glapion Legendre 1903.

Beginning with Marie Laveau and Christophe Glapion, I will explain how these individuals were connected to the Laveau-Glapion family and give the circumstances of their death. I will also discuss the family members who are *not* buried in the tomb–those who left New Orleans and those who stayed in the city but chose interment in other cemeteries. They are grouped together according to family relationships, not in chronological order of their birth or death.

MARIE LAVEAU AND CHRISTOPHE GLAPION

Marie Laveau died of natural causes in her home at 152 St. Ann on June 15, 1881, a few months short of her eightieth birthday. Such was her renown that remembrances and tributes appeared not only in the local newspapers but also in the *New York Times*. Most rejected the idea that Marie was actually a Voudou priestess, portraying her instead as a woman of great beauty, intellect, and charisma who was also pious, generous, and a skilled herbal healer.

The reporter for the *New Orleans City Item* wrote that "Few women were more charitable, few more kind, few more beloved than Marie Laveau," and that "whatever superstitious stories were whispered about her, it is at least certain that she enjoyed the respect and affection of thousands who knew her, of numbers whom she befriended in times of dire distress, of sick folks snatched from the shadow of death and nursed by her to health and strength." The *New Orleans Daily Picayune* spoke of her charity to the poor, who were "welcome to food and lodging at any time of night or day," and of her abilities as a yellow fever and cholera nurse and her knowledge of "the valuable healing qualities of indigenous herbs." Marie "labored incessantly" to comfort condemned prisoners, praying with them in their last moments and endeavoring to rescue them from the gallows. Echoing the New Orleans newspapers, the *New York Times* concluded that Marie Laveau was "one of the most wonderful women who ever lived," lamenting that "Now her lips are closed forever...and as she could neither read nor write, not a scrap is left to chronicle the events of her exciting life."[26]

Marie's funeral, conducted by Father Hyacinth Mignot of St. Louis

Cathedral, took place at 5:00 p.m. on June 16. The *Daily Picayune* obituary noted that "Her remains were followed to the grave by a large concourse of people, the most prominent and the most humble joining in paying their last respects to the dead," and related that Marie's "last days were spent surrounded by sacred pictures and other evidences of religion, and she died with a firm trust in heaven. While God's sunshine plays around the little tomb where her remains are buried, by the side of her second husband and her sons and daughters, Marie Laveau's name will not be forgotten in New Orleans." [27]

The Burial Book states (in English) that "Dame Christophe Glapion" was placed "in the family tomb of Vve Paris, middle vault" on June 16, 1881. Despite this concrete evidence, there are many who will venture to say only that Marie Laveau is "alleged" or "reputed" to be interred in the famous Widow Paris tomb.[28]

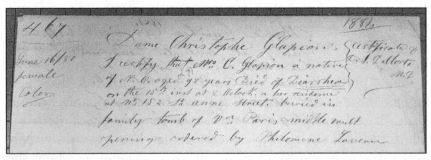

fig. 11: Burial Book entry for Dame Christophe Glapion (Marie Laveau), June 16, 1881, Burial Book 1881-1883, p. 467, courtesy of the Office of Archives and Records, Archdiocese of New Orleans. Note that the 1881-1883 records are included in the Burial Book for June-August 1873.

A persistent legend maintains that Marie was originally interred in the Widow Paris tomb in 1881, but that her family had her body moved to another location to avoid excessive attention from devotees and curiosity seekers. In the unlikely event that the Laveau-Glapion family actually transported Marie's body intact to another tomb, they would have done it before 1897, when Marie's baby great-granddaughters Clara Westenberg and Marie Legendre were placed in the middle vault. At that time, what was left of Marie's wooden coffin would have been discarded and her bones pushed to the back to mingle with the dust of earlier interments. There is no removal notation written over the "Dame Christophe Glapion" entry in the Burial Book. The Archdiocesan Cemeteries Office verified that "a body could never be moved without permission from the Archdiocese. They would have to open the vault and do the removal, and there would be a record of it."[29] The family *might* have moved Marie's body without permission from the Archdiocese, but their secretiveness would have defeated the alleged purpose of deflecting attention away from her burial place.

fig. 12: This wall vault in St. Louis Cemetery No. 2, Square 3, corner Iberville and Robertson, has long been reputed to be the "true" resting place of Marie Laveau. St. Louis No. 2 is not heavily visited by tourists and so far the Archdiocesan Cemeteries Office still allows unaccompanied access. Devotees sometimes leave flowers, notes, personal photographs, money, candles, rosaries, and religions images, and draw Xs. Photo by Carolyn Long, All Saints' Day, 1998.

fig. 13: This tomb, near the back of the cemetery, is said by some tour guides to be that of Marie Laveau, her daughter, or Doctor John, tomb No. 256 on the Dead Space map. There is no ownership record for this tomb. Photo courtesy of Mary Millan, Bloody Mary's Tours.

fig. 14: Another of the alleged "Marie Laveau tombs," on the aisle parallel to Conti Street, tomb No. 339 on the Dead Space map. Records show that this tomb actually belongs to the Alaux family and has no connection to Marie Laveau. Photo courtesy of Mary Millan, Bloody Mary's Tours.

Many people still nevertheless believe that Marie Laveau's true resting place is in the wall vault in St. Louis Cemetery No. 2, located in Square 3 in the Iberville Street wall near the corner of Robertson Street. In the earlier twentieth century this was called the "Wishing Vault" and was the site of considerable Voudou activity. Even today some devotees leave offerings and draw Xs at this site. Inquiries to the Archdiocesan Cemeteries Office uncovered no ownership record for this wall vault.[30]

By the 1990s some imaginative tour guides had adopted a couple of crumbling and abandoned tombs in St. Louis Cemetery No. 1, designating them as the "authentic" burial sites of Marie Laveau, of her alleged successor known as "Marie II," or of her contemporary, the African-born Voudou priest Jean Montanée, known as Doctor John. Xs and offerings also proliferated on these tombs. There is absolutely no documentation that either of these locations has any connection with the Laveau-Glapion family.

Marie's life partner, Christophe Glapion, predeceased her by twenty-six years. Christophe died at age sixty-six at the family residence on June 26, 1855, and was buried on June 27. His funeral announcement appeared in the *New Orleans Bee* of June 27, 1855: "His friends and acquaintances are asked to attend, without further invitation, at his burial, which will take place this evening at precisely five o'clock. The company will leave from his home at St. Ann Street between Burgundy and Rampart." There is no Burial Book for 1855, but I found Christophe in the register of St. Louis Cathedral Funeral Expenses for 1852-1855: *Enterrement de quatriesse classe de Christophe Dmy. de Glapion... Exposé rue Ste. Anne entre Bourgogne & Ramparts...enterrement cim^re No. 1* (fourth class burial of Christophe Duminy de Glapion.... Viewing at St. Ann Street between Burgundy and Rampart...burial in cemetery No. 1).[31] His name appears at the top of the middle tablet of the Widow Paris tomb as *Cphe Duminy De Glapion, décédé le 26 Juin 1855.* Not only had Marie lost her beloved companion, she and her family were plunged into a financial crisis from which they never fully recovered.[32]

THE LAVEAU-GLAPION CHILDREN

Of the seven children born to Marie and Christophe, all but Eloise Euchariste and Philomène died young. As we have seen, there are funeral records but no burial records for Marie Louise Caroline, Christophe, and Jean Baptiste. The others are either definitely or presumed to be interred in the Widow Paris tomb.

François Glapion, born on September 22, 1833, was buried on May 19, 1834. In the Burial Book for 1834-1835 he is described as *enfant d.c.l. agé de 8 mois né en cette Paroisse, fils de Mr Dominique Glapion et de Marie Laveaud f.d.c.l. ses père et mère* (free child of color aged eight months, son of Mr. Dominique (Christophe) Glapion and Marie Laveau free woman of color, his father and mother." François probably was laid to rest in the Widow Paris tomb, but since the early books give only minimal information, it is impossible to say this with certainty.

The previously mentioned Archange Glapion was born on June 5, 1838, and died on January 6, 1845.[33] The loss of this child, the only son to have survived infancy, must have been particularly tragic for Marie and Christophe. There is a civil death certificate for Archange, but no funeral register or Burial Book exists for 1845. His name and death date are inscribed below that of Christophe Glapion on the middle tablet and again on a marble slab set into the pavement: *Archange Glapion, mort en Jan 1845, 7 ans, 7 mois* (died in January 1845, seven years, seven months).

fig. 15: Marble inscription tablet for Archange Glapion and Joseph Eugène Crocker set into the pavement in front of the Widow Paris tomb.

THE GLAPION-CROCKER DESCENDANTS

Marie Eloise (Helöise) Euchariste Glapion was born on February 2, 1827, the first child of Marie Laveau and Christophe Glapion.[34] As one of Marie's two surviving daughters, Eloise Glapion is often cited as being her mother's successor. The notion of the mother-daughter duo, "Marie I" and "Marie II," was introduced in the 1920s.

It was most fully developed in Robert Tallant's 1946 book *Voodoo in New Orleans,* a flamboyant work replete with lurid tales of nudity, drunkenness, devil worship, snake handling, blood drinking, the devouring of live chickens and dead cats, and interracial sexual orgies. Tallant conflated Eloise and her younger sister Philomène into one woman called "Marie Glapion" or "Marie II."[35] As we will see, Eloise died in the early 1860s and could not have replaced her mother as "Queen of the Voudous."

fig. 16: The endpapers from the first 1946 edition of Robert Tallant's *Voodoo in New Orleans,* depict "naked savages" engaged in a "voodoo orgy." This exemplifies Tallant's sensationalistic portrayal of the Voudou religion. (Collection of Carolyn Long)

Eloise Glapion had a long-term relationship with Pierre Crokére (usually anglicized as Crocker or Croker), a successful free-colored commission broker, builder, and architect. Together they had five children between about 1844 and 1853. Pierre Crocker did not make his home with Eloise and their children at the Laveau-Glapion household on St. Ann. He lived on St. Philip Street with his legal wife, Rose Gignac, and fathered children with Rose while also consorting with Eloise. Eloise Glapion's death date is controversial. In 1881 her only surviving son, Victor Pierre Crocker, opened her succession in probate court because he required authority to sell her property. He testified that his mother had died in June 1862.[36] When researching my 2006 Laveau biography, *A New Orleans Voudou Priestess,* I found no civil death certificate, coroner's report, newspaper announcement, funeral notice, or burial record to substantiate that date, but attributed this to the turmoil caused by the Union takeover of New Orleans in April 1862.

Still puzzling over Eloise's death date, I was excited to discover in the Burial Book for 1859-1864 a record for "Madame Widow Oscar, *née* Glapion," a thirty-four-year-old free woman of color who died of tuberculosis on July 19, 1860, at the Laveau-Glapion home. The next day her body was placed in the upper vault of the Widow Paris tomb.[37] Her age, date and place of death, and the site of her interment raise the intriguing possibility that she could be Eloise Euchariste Glapion. After twenty-one years, did Victor Pierre Crocker incorrectly recall the date of his mother's death when he opened her succession?

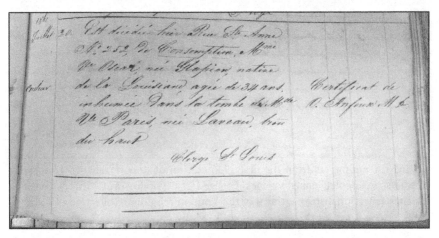

fig. 17: Burial Book entry for Madame Widow Oscar *née* Glapion (possibly Marie Laveau's daughter Eloise Glapion), July 20, 1860, Burial Book 1859-1864, p. 103. Courtesy of the Office of Archives and Records, Archdiocese of New Orleans.

But what are we to make of this lady being identified as "Madame Widow Oscar"? As with the search for Eloise Glapion's death record, a search for "Widow Oscar" under every possible variation of her name produced no other documentation of her death—or of *any* woman of color who died on July 19, 1860. The mystery is deepened by the fact that Eloise's daughter Onesta Crocker, discussed below, was sometimes called Onesta Oscar Mansini. Did Eloise have a relationship with a man named Oscar Mansini after Pierre Crocker died in 1857? A search for Oscar Mansini also produced no results, and this remains another of the unsolved puzzles surrounding the Laveau-Glapion family.

Eloise Glapion's first two children with Pierre Crocker died young. Joseph Eugène Crocker was born February 28, 1844, and died at the age of eleven months on May 5, 1845.[38] His sister Esmeralda Crocker, for whom we have no birth date, died on January 8, 1850. There is no burial record for either of these children, but their names are inscribed, along with those of Christophe and Archange Glapion, on the middle tablet of the Widow Paris tomb: *Jph. Eugène Crocker décédé le 5 Mais 1845/ Esmeralda Crocker décédé le 8 Janvier 1850.* Joseph Eugène's name also appears, along with that of Archange Glapion, on the marble slab set into the pavement. Three other Crocker children, Aldina, Onesta, and Victor Pierre, survived to adulthood and grew up in the Laveau-Glapion household at 152 St. Ann, where they were enumerated in the census for 1850, 1860, and 1870.[39]

Adelai Aldina Crocker was born to Eloise Glapion and Pierre Crocker on December 25, 1847, and baptized as Adelai Glapion.[40] She was called "Malvina" in the 1850 census, "Alzonia" in the 1860 census, and "Alina" in the 1870 census. She never married and had no known children. On September 9, 1871, she died at age twenty-six of "abscess of the liver" at 152 St. Ann. The Burial Book entry refers to her as A. Aldina Croker, *petit fille* (granddaughter) *de Marie Laveau dit Madame Parisse.* The next day she was *inhume dans la voute du haut tombe de famille Parise ou Marie Laveau* (interred in the upper vault of the tomb of the family Parise or Marie Laveau."[41]

Adelai's younger sister, Marguerite Onesta (or Honesta) Crocker, was born July 12, 1849, and baptized as "Marie Glapious." She was called "Honesta" in the 1850 census and "Amazone" in the 1860 census.[42] While doing research for *A New Orleans Voudou Priestess,* it seemed that this girl had disappeared from the record after 1860. The mystery was solved by the publication of Barbara Trevigne's awesomely documented article, "Ball of Confusion: Célestin Glapion and the Glapion Family of Louisiana," in the October 2010 issue of *New Orleans Genesis*. Trevigne's research revealed that in 1868 Onesta had married Alexis Célestin Glapion. The civil marriage certificate called her "Marie Marguerite Mansini," and the marriage record in the sacramental register of St. Louis Cathedral identified her as "Marguerite Onesta Crocker, daughter of Pierre Crocker and Eucharis (Eloise Euchariste) Glapion."[43] The couple is listed in the 1870 census as Célestin and Honesta "Glapillon," residing in the Laveau-Glapion household.[44]

Alexis Célestin Glapion was descended from Christophe Glapion's great-uncle, Jean Baptiste Duminy de Glapion, and an enslaved woman named Lizette. Lizette and her children, Marie and Célestin, were manumitted by Jean Baptiste de Glapion and went on to live productive lives in New Orleans.[45] Célestin Glapion was a skilled cabinetmaker, and his male descendants worked in the building trades.[46] No member of this branch of the Glapion family fits the description of the woman identified as "Madame Widow Oscar née Glapion" who died in 1860.

Onesta and her husband Alexis Célestin appear to have had two children together. A two-month-old boy named Henry Raphael Glapion died of "maramus infantitis" at 152 St. Ann on September 14, 1873. His body was placed in the middle vault of the tomb of Mme Veuve Paris. An infant named Antoine Raphael (no surname) died of "general debility" on October 17, 1874. The baby was stated on the interment record to have died "at his mother's residence on St. Ann Street No. 152 between Burgundy and Rampart." Like Henry Raphael, Antoine Raphael was placed in the middle vault of the tomb of Mme Veuve Paris dit Marie Laveau.[47] Neither the civil death certificates nor the interment records named the parents of these children, but they were almost certainly the sons of Onesta Crocker and Alexis Célestin Glapion. Because all of Marie Laveau and Christophe Glapion's sons died young, none of their direct descendants are named Glapion. If Henry and Antoine had lived, they would have carried on the Glapion surname as direct male descendants.

Onesta Crocker Glapion, age twenty-seven, died of tuberculosis at 152 St. Ann on November 22, 1876. Her civil death certificate gives her name as "Onesta Oscar Mansini." This brings to mind the 1860 interment record for Madame Widow Oscar, *née* Glapion, possibly

Onesta's mother, Eloise Euchariste Glapion. Onesta was interred in the upper vault of the tomb *portant inscription Famille Vve Paris* (bearing inscription Family of the Widow Paris), and the opening was *ordannée par Marie Laveau* (ordered by Marie Laveau).[48]

Less than a year later, Alexis Célestin Glapion married Emma Vicknaire and with her had many sons and daughters. He also had children with Victoria Perez and Josephine Valentine.[49] Although all of them have the Glapion surname, they are not descendants of Marie Laveau and Christophe Glapion.

The last of Eloise Glapion and Pierre Crocker's children was Victor Pierre Crocker. Unlike his siblings, Victor Pierre has no baptismal record. He testified, when opening his mother's succession, that he was born November 8, 1853, and baptized privately at 152 St. Ann. As an adult, Victor Pierre worked as a barber and used the names John or Peter Crocker, Croquoir, or Croker. He lived off and on in the Laveau-Glapion household on St. Ann Street.[50] In 1887 he married Catherine Teche.[51] Five years later, at age forty, he died of peritonitis on August 13, 1892. Victor Pierre had apparently been distancing himself from his African ancestry; he was classified as white on his civil death certificate and on the burial record. Victor Pierre's widow was enumerated in the census for 1900, where it was stated that she had no living children.[52]

Thus we know that the Glapion-Crocker line ended with Aldina, Onesta, and Victor Pierre, and that any direct descendants of Marie Laveau and Christophe Glapion come from the line produced by Philomène Glapion and her partner Alexandre Legendre.

THE GLAPION-LEGENDRE DESCENDANTS

Marie Philomène Glapion was born to Marie Laveau and Christophe Glapion on March 6, 1836. She was their last surviving child.[53] Philomène's life partner was a white man named Emile Alexandre Legendre, and she went by the name Madame Legendre. Interestingly, Alexandre Legendre was legally married to Judith Toutant Beauregard, sister of the famous Civil War general Pierre Gustave Toutant Beauregard. By 1850 Judith had departed for New York with their three children and spent the rest of her life there.[54] Philomène and Alexandre began their relationship around 1855. They lived together at 362 Dauphine between what are now Kerlerec and Pauger streets in the Faubourg Marigny. This cottage, now numbered 1820 Dauphine, still stands. Their seven children were born there between 1857 and 1870.

Three of the Legendre children died in infancy. Eugénie succumbed to "infant debility" shortly after her birth in 1866. Twin boys, Etienne Joseph St. Marc and Charles St. Marc, were born February 10, 1870. Joseph expired the next day, and Charles died five months later. Their three little bodies were all placed "in the upper vault of the tomb bearing the inscription Madame Paris *née* Laveau."[55] The other Legendre children, Fidelia, Alexandre, Noëmie, and Blair, survived to adulthood. Only Alexandre, who died in 1903, is buried in the Widow Paris tomb.

Philomène's partner Alexandre Legendre died in 1872, and his white relatives took charge of his interment in St. Louis Cemetery No. 3.[56] Philomène and her children returned to the Laveau-Glapion family home. She was only thirty-six years old at the time and identified herself as a widow.

From 1872 until Marie Laveau died in 1881, Philomène was her mother's caregiver. Marie Laveau's deteriorating health is confirmed by testimony that she gave in 1873 related to the succession of a family friend. A justice of the peace came to the Laveau-Glapion home on St. Ann Street, where Marie stated that she was "about seventy years old.... I am sick for some time past. I am too sick to leave my room and cannot walk."[57] Philomène cared for her mother until Marie died in 1881, and continued to live at 152 St. Ann with her adult children, the children of her deceased sister Eloise Euchariste Glapion, and many grandchildren.[58]

In the years following Marie Laveau's death, Philomène was besieged by curious newspaper men investigating the legacy of the "Voudou Queen." In 1886, a *New Orleans Daily Picayune* reporter visited the cottage on St. Ann Street, where he encountered Philomène with other female family members. He noted that "every one of the group was comely," especially Madame Legendre, who "although her heavy mass of hair is turning as white as that of her mother, still shows the signs of beauty that she inherited. Tall, majestic, graceful, the eye still flashing fire, and with firm step notwithstanding months of illness, she rules her household, even if she has not the tact of Marie Laveau to extend her realm and number her subjects by the hundreds." Another *Picayune* reporter came calling in 1890, and described Madame Legendre as "a splendid specimen of womanhood. Her eyes are large, dark, and dreamy, and when lit up by excitement shine with a wonderful light; a mass of snow-white hair crowns her head and she is queenly and majestic in her bearing." The piece ends by declaring that Madame Legendre "never had any connection" with Voudou, and that she "maintained her mother's old home for the sake of a happy and memorable past."[59]

Fidelia Alexandre Legendre was born November 17, 1857.[60] Fidelia was Philomène's older daughter and had always been her mother's mainstay. In 1890, at the rather advanced age (for that time) of thirty-three, Fidelia married Julius Westenberg, a native of Germany. The Reconstruction-era civil code enacted in 1870 legalized interracial marriage, and only in 1894 did the law revert to restricting marriage to couples of the same race. Fidelia and her husband departed for St. Louis, and their children, Anna, Julius Jr., and Clara, were born there between 1890 and 1897. The entire family identified as white.[61]

Philomène's younger daughter, Noëmie Marguerite Legendre, was born October 10, 1862.[62] In 1880, ten years before Fidelia's marriage to Julius Westenberg, Noëmie also married a white man, John Benjamin Santenac.[63] Noëmie and Benjamin had three children, Benjamin Alexander, Antoinette, and Marita, before they separated and Noëmie moved back to the Laveau-Glapion home.[64] Tragically, both daughters died in 1894. Antoinette Santenac, ten years old, was accidentally drowned while on a Sunday afternoon outing near Lake Pontchartrain. The *New Orleans Daily Picayune* of September 17 carried an article explaining that the child, a resident of 152 St. Ann, had "missed her footing while crossing the trestle of the bridge at the intersection of the Orleans Canal and Spanish Fort Road, fell into the canal, and was drowned. The body was recovered shortly after and conveyed to the city on the Spanish Fort train, and thence removed to the morgue in the patrol wagon.... The remains were taken in charge by the girl's relatives." Antoinette was interred "in the family tomb of Marie Laveau, upper vault." The opening was ordered by her uncle, Alexandre Legendre.[65] A few months later, on December 7, eight-year-old Marita Santenac died of typhoid fever at 152 St. Ann. She was interred in the same vault as her sister Antoinette, with the opening again being ordered by her uncle.[66]

Philomène's son Alexandre Glapion Legendre (called Alex), was born May 8, 1859.[67] Alex Legendre made his living as a dealer in wild game. In 1885 he married a woman of color, Mathilde Lachapelle, and with her had one child named Blair Manuel, born in 1887.[68] While legally married to Mathilde, Alex began a relationship with another woman of color, Ernestine Llado, and with her returned to the family home on St. Ann Street. Alex and Ernestine had six children: Arthur, Ernest, Amelie, François Pierre, Pauline, and Marie, born between 1885 and 1897 at 152 St. Ann.[69] Amelie, born in 1890, died April 3, 1896, but surprisingly there is no record of her being buried in the Widow Paris tomb.[70]

The spring and summer of 1897 was a tragic time for the Laveau-Glapion family. First Ernestine Llado died at age thirty-two on March 26, 1897. The cause of death was given as tuberculosis, but she almost certainly died giving birth to her daughter Marie. Ernestine was interred "in the family tomb of Philomène Glapion lower vault."[71] Fidelia Legendre Westenberg, with her husband and family, had returned to New Orleans from St. Louis to care for Fidelia's mother Philomène. On April 5 their four-month-old daughter Clara Westenberg died of cholera at the family home. She was interred "in Madame Legendre's family tomb, middle vault." The opening was ordered by the baby's aunt, Noëmie Legendre.[72] Then Alex and Ernestine's twenty-one-day-old daughter, Marie Legendre, died of "marasmus" on April 16. She was placed next to little Clara Westenberg "in Madame Legendre's tomb middle vault."[73]

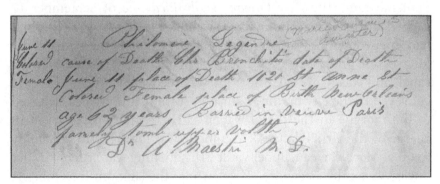

fig. 18: Burial Book entry for Philomène Glapion Legendre, June 11, 1897, Burial Book 1893-1900, p. 189. Courtesy of the Office of Archives and Records, Archdiocese of New Orleans.

Philomène Glapion Legendre, age sixty-two, died at home on June 11, 1897. By then the street numbering had changed, and the address was given as 1020 St. Ann Street. The cause was reported as chronic bronchitis, but like Ernestine Laddo and other family members and friends, she might have been suffering from tuberculosis.[74] She was interred in the top vault of the Widow Paris tomb.

Beneath the designation Famille Vve. Paris née Laveau, the inscription on the marble tablet reads:

> *Ci-Git*
> *Marie Philomé Glapion*
> *décédée le 11 Juin 1897*
> *Agée de Soixante-deux ans*
> *Elle fut bonne mère, bonne amie, et*
> *regrettée par tous ceux qui l'ont connue*
> *Passant priez pour elle.*

(Here lies Marie Philomé Glapion, died June 11, 1897, aged sixty-two years. She was a good mother, a good friend, and regretted by all who knew her. Passers-by pray for her.)

fig. 19: This inscription for Marie Philomè Glapion appears on the upper vault of the Widow Paris tomb, below the title *Famille Vve Paris née Laveau.*

THE DARCANTEL-GONDRON-EASTIN DESCENDANTS

In addition to the children, grandchildren, and great-grandchildren of Marie Laveau and Christophe Glapion, two of Marie's grand-nephews were interred in the Widow Paris tomb. Both were the children of Louise Pauline Gondron and Edouard Ransom Eastin. Louise Pauline was the daughter of Marie's maternal half-sister, Marie Louise Darcantel, with her white partner Joseph Derozin Gondron. Pauline and her family, including her brother, Derozin Gondron, were living at least some of the time in the Laveau-Glapion household.

On September 9, 1860, Edouard Eastin, age six, died of diphtheria, and was placed in the family tomb (no vault was specified).[75] Edouard is recorded in the Burial Book for 1859-1864 as *fils de E. Easten et de dame Louisa Gendran, inhumé dans la tombe de Mde Vve Paris* (son of E. Easten [*sic*] and Dame Louisa Gendran [*sic*], buried in the tomb of Madame Widow Paris). There is no record for Edouard's brother Eugène Eastin (born July 24, 1856, died September 6, 1857) because

fig. 20: This inscription tablet for Edouard and Eugène Eastin must have once been attached to the Widow Paris tomb. At some point it was probably removed and, as was customary, was propped against the side of the tomb. Cemetery authorities later embedded it in a large cement slab in St. Louis Cemetery No. 1, alley No. 7, along with other tablets gathered together in order to preserve them. Photo courtesy of Kevin Servat.

44

there is no Burial Book for 1857. We can assume that Eugène was also laid to rest in the family tomb because a marble inscription tablet bearing the names and dates of Edouard and Eugène is embedded in a cement slab in St. Louis Cemetery No. 1, alley No. 7, along with other tablets gathered together in order to preserve them.[76]

It was sometimes customary, when new interments were added to a tomb, to replace the existing inscription tablet and prop the old one against the side. This can still be seen on some tombs, but it leaves the loose tablets vulnerable to theft and breakage. The tablet for Archange Glapion and Joseph Eugène Crocker was probably "rescued" and embedded into the pavement in front of the Widow Paris tomb for the same reason.

Besides these twenty-five family members, we will see that a number of other people--slaves, friends, neighbors, and strangers—were interred in the Widow Paris tomb.

SLAVES

The Burial Books record the burial of two slaves in the Widow Paris tomb. A black man named Jean Louis, age sixty-nine, described as the "slave of Marie Laveau Vve Paris," was interred January 9, 1835. This early book does not specify the location of the tomb. Marie, "negresse slave of Mme Marie Laveau," died of old age and was interred October 29, 1861, "in the tomb of Marie Laveau Vve Paris, lower vault."[77] Marie Laveau and Christophe Glapion are documented to have owned eight slaves, but there is no record of their acquiring Jean Louis and Marie.[78]

FRIENDS

Eight of the people interred in the Widow Paris tomb can be identified as friends of the Laveau-Glapion family.

MONETTE

Pierre Monette was a free man of color who had emigrated from Haiti in the early nineteenth century. Marie Laveau and Christophe Glapion had social and business dealings with Monette over the years, and he served as legal guardian to their granddaughter Onesta Crocker after both her parents passed away.[79] Pierre Monette died at age seventy-eight of "cerebral congestive fever" on April 24, 1872, and was placed in the middle vault of the tomb of Mme *Veuve Paris dit Marie Laveau.* Pierre's newborn grandson, Charles Albert Monette, died a few weeks later on March 11, 1872, and was laid in the upper vault. Then on August 11, 1872, Pierre's twenty-four-year-old daughter-in-law, referred to only as Mme Edouard Monette, died of tuberculosis and was interred in the lower vault of the tomb of Mme Veuve Paris.[80] Interestingly, a granddaughter of Pierre Monette, Louise Hermance Monette, became the mother of Ferdinand Joseph Lamothe–known to the world as Jelly Roll Morton.[81] The Monette tomb is directly across the aisle from the Widow Paris tomb.

ADAMS

Two members of the family of Judge Lucien Adams were laid to rest in the Widow Paris tomb. Lucien Adams, a white man, was a well-known New Orleans character who was an attorney, judge, and chief of police during his long career. He was born in Terrebonne Parish in 1820 and died in New Orleans at age seventy-nine in 1900. His obituary in the *New Orleans Daily Picayune* described him as "always neat and tidy in his attire, and he invariably appeared in a snow-white linen suit. He had a straight back and was stoutly built [with] not a wrinkle in his face, although the years had liberally sprinkled his hair with silver threads."[82]

Robert Tallant alluded to Judge Adams in his 1946 book *Voodoo in New Orleans.* We have observed that Tallant promoted the notion that as Marie Laveau grew older, she was succeeded as leader of the Voudou congregation by her daughter, "Marie II," a conflation of Eloise and Philomène Glapion. Tallant claimed that "Marie II" was the friend, and perhaps the mistress, of a "notable attorney" who New Orleanians of the time readily identified as Lucien Adams: "For years [he] was in her employ [as her attorney], and she is said to have advised him as much as he advised her." In a later passage, Tallant added that "Marie II had many lovers, both white and colored. At least several of them were prominent men of the city, one being a rather distinguished judge."[83] Tallant is notorious for his preposterous inventions, but some of these statements are loosely based on interviews conducted by the Louisiana Writers' Project. Echoing the description in Judge Adams' *Daily Picayune* obituary, one woman said that: "Judge Lucien Adams lived over on Rampart Street at Dumaine. He surely was a fine man and fine looking too. He was always dressed in white--look like a fresh suit every day." This informant went on to note that Judge Adams "went to [Marie Laveau's] house every morning on his way to his office. He was her lawyer." Another said that Marie Laveau engineered Lucien Adams' promotion to chief of police.[84]

Archival evidence shows that Lucien Adams indeed had a long-standing friendship with Marie Laveau and her daughter Philomène. On the evening of April 6, 1876, Judge Adams and his twenty-seven-year-old son Lucien Jr. were involved in a "bloody fracas" at a meeting of the Southern Republican Club at the Mechanics Hall. The judge, his son, and another man were wounded by gunfire. Lucien Jr. died the next day.[85] At that time Lucien Sr. was judge of the Fourth Municipal Police Court and Lucien Jr. was clerk of that same court. A Burial Book entry states that on April 7, 1876, Lucien Joseph Adams Jr., was placed in the lower vault of the *tombe portant inscription D. Bienvenu allée du centre* (tomb bearing inscription of D. Bienvenu center aisle). This tomb belonged to Lucien Jr.'s maternal great-grandfather, Alexandre Devince Bienvenu. Young Lucien was subsequently moved to the Widow Paris tomb. The notation written perpendicularly across the Burial Book entry states that *le corps a été transferé dans la tombe a seconde allée a droite, tombe achétée de Philomène Laveau* (the body was transferred to the tomb, second aisle on the right, tomb under the control of [literally "purchased by"] Philomène Laveau).[86]

fig. 21: Burial Book entry for Lucien Adams Jr., April 7, 1876, Burial Book 1874-1881, p. 168, courtesy of the Office of Archives and Records, Archdiocese of New Orleans. This shows the typical notation, written perpendicularly across the entry, which records the removal of a body from one tomb to another.

On May 6, 1881, the month before Marie Laveau's death, Judge Adams' mother-in-law, Charlotte Virginie Bienvenu, Widow of Charles Fagot, died at age seventy-eight of "softening of the brain." Like Lucien Adams Jr., the Widow Fagot was originally laid in the Bienvenu family tomb. But again a notation written over the Burial Book entry states that "the body was transferred to the tomb *achétée de Philomène Laveau.*"[87]

Why were the bodies of Lucien Adams Jr. and the Widow Fagot moved from the tomb of their Bienvenu ancestors to that of Marie Laveau? An intriguing statement appears in an interview conducted by the Louisiana Writers' Project, in which an elderly African American man said that the Widow Paris tomb originally belonged to the Adams family.[88] This perception is also held by descendants of Judge Lucien Adams. According to family lore, the cemetery plots on which the Adams tomb and the Widow Paris tomb now stand were both purchased by Judge Adams' father in 1819, and he may have commissioned the building of both tombs.[89] My attempts to verify this information through the Archdiocesan Cemeteries Office were unsuccessful.

The statement that Judge Adams was "Marie Laveau's lawyer" has some basis in fact. The financial well-being of the Laveau-Glapion family began to decline after Christophe Glapion's death in 1855, and by the late 1880s, after Marie had also died, Philomène and her children and grandchildren were experiencing hard times. In 1886 the State of Louisiana impounded the St. Ann Street cottage for unpaid taxes, and Philomène's daughter Fidelia Legendre had to redeem it for the amount owed. Notarial records show that the family was represented by Lucien Adams.[90]

Is there anything that might substantiate Tallant's inference that "Marie II" was the lover of Judge Lucien Adams? In early February 1876, shortly before Philomène ordered the transfer of the body of Lucien Adams Jr. to the Widow Paris tomb, a baby named Manuel Legendre was born at 152 St. Ann. On May 9, 1876, Manuel died there from "inflammation of the intestines" and was buried in the upper vault of the tomb "bearing the inscription Famille Vve Paris."[91] The civil death certificate describes the baby as "the lawful issue of Hermogene Legendre with Philomène Dauphine." These names did not turn up in a search of archival sources, and I suspect that they were invented to conceal the identity of the parents. Although admittedly farfetched, is it possible that Judge Adams was visiting Philomène "every morning on his way to his office" for more than giving and receiving legal advice? Could Manuel Legendre have been Philomène's child with Lucien Adams?

LLADO

We have seen that Ernestine Llado was the domestic partner of Marie Laveau's grandson Alex Legendre, and that she was interred in the lower vault of the Widow Paris tomb. Two men who were probably Ernestine's brothers were also buried in the family tomb. Charles Ernest Llado was interred in the lower vault on June 13, 1887. Joseph Llado was also placed in the lower vault on April 8, 1910. City directories show that Joseph lived off and on at the Laveau-Glapion home between 1879 and 1892. A three-year-old girl named Delphine Llado was laid in the lower vault on January 22, 1885; her relationship to the family of Ernestine Llado is unclear.[92]

NEIGHBORS

The Burial Books and civil death certificates often gave the home address or place of death of the deceased.[93] Three people who were not related to the Laveau-Glapion family actually died at 152 St. Ann. A one-year-old child of color, Antoine Cuney, succumbed to cholera there in 1869; he might have been one of Marie Laveau's patients. In the 1890s, after Marie had died, two more people of color expired at 152 St. Ann. Pauline Vigne, age seventy-five, died of "senile debility" in 1892, and Albert Becknou, age thirty-five, died of alcoholism in 1894.[94] Philomène, continuing her mother's charitable work, might have been caring for them.

Six others who were interred in the Widow Paris tomb lived and died nearby in the Vieux Carré, and one was a neighbor of Philomène Glapion Legendre when she lived on Dauphine Street before 1873. We can assume that Marie or Philomène knew these people and offered use of their family tomb when needed in an emergency. A French immigrant tinsmith, Dominique Moreau, died in 1870 of yellow fever on Bourbon between St. Ann and Dumaine. Corine Ayala, a ten-year-old white native of Havana, died of tuberculosis on North Rampart between St. Ann and Dumaine in 1874. John Eaton, native of Vermont, died of a hemorrhage on North Rampart between Dumaine and St. Philip in 1877. Eight-month-old Leliha Fegue, a child of color, died of convulsions in 1878 at St. Ann corner of Burgundy, just a few doors away from the Laveau-Glapion home. Lucie Billard, a four-year-old white child, died of yellow fever in 1878 at the corner of Chartres and Bienville. In 1889, Joseph McLean, an eight-year-old child of color, died of diphtheria on St. Ann between Royal and Bourbon. Etienne Felix, a forty-year-old man of color who lived next door to Philomène Glapion and Alexandre Legendre on Dauphine Street, died of cancer in 1870.[95]

RENTALS

Seven of the interments in the Widow Paris tomb were the result of rentals that were meant to be temporary but almost always ended up being permanent. Between 1872 and 1879 the Burial Books contain seven records of the Widow Paris tomb being rented. It is unknown whether or not Marie Laveau was acquainted with these families.

In 1872, seven-month-old Caroline Julien died of bronchitis. Caroline was the daughter of Charles Julien, a free-colored laborer living on Burgundy Street in the Faubourg Marigny, who "for the consideration of $15 rented a space for one year in the lower vault without marble owned by Madame Paris." A white child named Ida Durand died of meningitis in 1873, and was also interred in the lower vault. The burial space was rented for a year by her father, Alexander Durand, a carpenter residing on St. Louis between Marais and Villere. The 1873 interment record for Henriette Lameyer, a forty-year-old woman of color who died uptown on Erato Street, specified that she was placed in the upper vault of the Widow Paris tomb "rented for one year with condition of renewal and transport of corpse to its proper place." Felix Michel Gaudet, a white baby, died of pneumonia at the corner St. Louis and North Rampart in 1878. His father, Charles Gaudet, a physician and druggist, rented burial space in the upper vault of the Widow Paris tomb.[96] In two cases the rental was arranged by Manuel Cauvain, sexton of St. Louis Cemetery No. 1 in the 1870s and possibly a friend of Marie Laveau. Henry Gusman, a white baby, was interred in 1878, "in the lower vault of the tomb bearing inscription Vve Paris." Angela Sapata, a seventeen-year-old native of Mexico, was placed "in the middle vault of the tomb of the Family Widow Paris" in 1879.[97]

In only one instance was there evidence that a body had been moved to its final destination. Lucien Gex, age fifty-nine, a native of Savoie, France, owned a lime and plaster business on Basin Street between St. Louis and Toulouse, undoubtedly providing these materials for use at the nearby St. Louis Cemetery No. 1. When he died in 1876, his representatives rented the middle vault of the Widow Paris tomb. A notation written over the Burial Book entry states that his remains were "moved to St. Jacques, June 6, 1877, ordered by renter of the tomb." There is no St. Jacques Cemetery in New Orleans–perhaps his body was returned to France.[98]

THE LAVEAU-GLAPION FAMILY
AND THE WIDOW PARIS TOMB
AFTER 1897

Everything changed for the Laveau-Glapion family after 1897. Philomène Glapion Legendre had become the family matriarch after Marie Laveau died. When Philomène passed away on June 11, 1897, the clan began to disperse.

On September 24, 1897, Philomène's younger daughter Noëmie Legendre Santenac sold the family home for $1,000.[99] This property had belonged to their ancestors since 1798, and had sheltered Marie Laveau's grandmother and mother, Marie and her partner Christophe Glapion, their children, grandchildren, great-grandchildren, and other relatives and friends. With this sale the old St. Ann Street cottage passed out of the Laveau-Glapion family. It was torn down in 1903 and replaced by the double shotgun house that now stands at 1020-1022 St. Ann.

The entire South had undergone tremendous social upheavals following the end of the Civil War, the abolition of slavery, and the legislation of the Reconstruction era that supposedly gave equal rights to all. New Orleans was engulfed by a backlash of racism that resulted in a rigid segregation previously unknown in the city. Many light-complexioned people of mixed race, descended from the former elite free-colored class, refused to endure this indignity. Some moved north and identified as white, and some who remained in New Orleans also changed their racial designation.

After helping to settle the family's financial affairs, Philomène's older daughter Fidelia Legendre Westenberg returned with her husband to St. Louis, Missouri. Fidelia had not only lost her mother, she had lost her baby daughter to cholera in New Orleans. The next year, on December 29, 1898, Fidelia died at age forty-one of "posterior spinal sclerosis" and was buried in St. Louis. She was designated as white on her civil death certificate; to hide her identity as an Afro-

Creole of Louisiana, the date and place of birth and the names and birthplaces of her parents were left blank. In 1903 Fidelia's husband Julius Westenberg married a German woman, was again widowed in 1917, and thereafter shared a home with his daughter Anna, Anna's husband Frank Schmidt, and their children Frank and Virginia.[100] This branch of the Laveau-Glapion family was absorbed into St. Louis's white German-American community.

By around 1900 Noëmie Legendre Santenac had moved to Louisville, Kentucky. There she entered into a relationship with a white man of German descent, John Zoller. No record of Noëmie divorcing her husband Benjamin Santenac or actually marrying Zoller has been located. The 1910 census for Louisville shows Noëmie's son, Benjamin Alexander Santenac, and her niece and nephew, Pauline and François Pierre (known as Frank) Legendre, living with the Zollers. Like Fidelia and her children, this branch of the family denied their Afro-Louisiana heritage. Noëmie claimed to be born in Canada, and variously gave her mother's birthplace as France or "at sea." Pauline and Frank Legendre claimed their mother (Ernestine Llado) was born in Spain or Mexico. By 1920, Benjamin's son, Emile John Santenac, and Pauline's daughter, Ernestine Noëmie Baize, were living in the Zoller household. Frank Legendre established his own home, and he and his wife and children, Francis, Ernestine, and Mary Catherine Legendre, were enumerated in the 1930 census for Louisville.[101] Noëmie Legendre Zoller died of a cerebral hemorrhage in Louisville at age seventy-one on March 11, 1934, and is buried there.[102]

Unlike Fidelia and Noëmie, Philomène's sons Alex and Blair Legendre stayed in New Orleans and identified as African American.

Alex Legendre made his living as a dealer in wild game, and lived most of his life in the Laveau-Glapion family home on St. Ann Street. Alex died of "abscess of the lungs" on January 7, 1903, and his body was placed with that of his life partner, Ernestine Llado, in the lower vault of the Widow Paris tomb.[103] They are the only two family members in the lower vault.

Blair Manuel Legendre, Alex's legitimate son with his wife Matilde Lachapelle, identified as African American, as did Blair Manuel's children, Rodney, Mabel, and Leonard Blair Legendre. Blair Manuel's death date is unknown. Rodney served in the U.S. Navy in WWII and died in Los Angeles; the others lived and died in New Orleans but none of them are buried in the Widow Paris tomb.[104]

The children that Alex Legendre had with Ernestine Llado, those who migrated to Louisville (Pauline and Frank) and those who remained in New Orleans (Arthur and Ernest), identified as white. Little is known about Arthur Legendre. He was enumerated in the 1910 census living in the home of his uncle Blair Legendre, after which he disappears from the archival record.[105] Ernest Legendre lived in New Orleans, had three children with his wife Violet Caubert, and died in 1948.[106] Their son Theodore Legendre lived and died in New Orleans. Their other children, Thomas Ernest and Ethel Claire Legendre (later Karl), settled in Bay St. Louis, Hancock County, Mississippi and died and were buried there.[107] I have been unable to locate evidence of children born to Alex's descendants who stayed in the New Orleans area.

Blair Arthur Legendre, born October 18, 1868, was the youngest son of Philomène Glapion and Alexandre Legendre.[108] Blair had a long-term relationship with Rose Camille, born in Mexico to Afro-Creole parents who had emigrated from New Orleans to Tampico. Blair and Rose had one son, Cyril John Legendre.[109] Blair worked as a house painter, living with Rose, Rose's sons Ferdinand and Gustave, and their own son Cyril. During the early years of the twentieth century, Blair and Rose Legendre were the only family members looking after the Widow Paris tomb and the Basin Street wall vault (the tomb on the St. Louis aisle had not been used since 1886). In 1940, interviewers from the Louisiana Writers' Project were told by the sexton of St. Louis Cemetery No. 1 that "an old woman named Rose Legendre came regularly to clean the tomb, claiming to be the widow of Blair Legendre, a grandson of Marie Laveau." Writers' Project workers sought out and interviewed Rose Camille Legendre and her son Cyril. Rose said that she cared for the tomb and removed the cross marks; she shared some memories of Marie Laveau and informed the interviewers that her husband Blair had died in 1932.[110]

Rose Legendre was designated as a widow in the 1940 New Orleans census, and listed as the contact person on her son Cyril's World War II draft registration card in 1942.[111] One would have expected Blair and Rose to be laid to rest in the family tomb, but they simply disappear from civil and church documents. A search of all available sources has not turned up a record of their death and burial in New Orleans or elsewhere. Cyril Legendre last appeared in the New Orleans city directory in 1945. Sometime after that he left for Los Angeles; he died and was buried there in 1965.[112] He had no known children.

There were only a few more interments in the family-owned burial sites after 1897. The Burial Books of this later period did not always indicate who ordered the opening, but when this information was included, it was Blair Legendre. Between 1901 and 1910 there were three more interments in the Basin Street wall vault.[113] Six more people were placed in the Widow Paris tomb: Alex Legendre (the last family member to be interred there) in 1903, Joseph Llado (probably Ernestine's brother) in 1910, and three older African American women who may have been friends or neighbors of Blair and Rose. After the final burial in 1917, that tomb was also abandoned.[114]

After forty years of inactivity, a final interment appeared in the Burial Book for 1921-1973. A sixty-nine-year-old African American woman named Bertha Alcindor (née Duplessis) died on August 15, 1957, and was interred August 20 in the "Archange Glapion tomb, lot #9 (7) alley 2 left facing St. Louis Street (lower vault) folio #95." There was no indication of who ordered the opening of the tomb.[115]

A funeral notice appeared in the *New Orleans Times-Picayune* of August 19, 1957:

> ALCINDOR–of 2515 St. Philip Street [between Rocheblave and Dorgenois], Sunday, August 15, 1957, at 12:15 o'clock a.m. MRS. BERTHA ALCINDOR. Relatives and friends of the family are respectfully invited to attend the wake services on Monday night, August 19, 1957, at the Carr and Llopis Mortuary, 1626 Dumaine Street near North Claiborne Avenue from whence the funeral will take place on Tuesday, August 20, 1957, at 3:30 o'clock p.m. Requiem mass at St. Peter Claver Church 1922 St. Philip Street. Interment in St. Louis No. 1 Cemetery. Carr and Llopis Mortuary in charge.[116]

According to her civil death certificate, Bertha Alcindor, a "domestic," died of coronary occlusion at Charity Hospital. The death was reported by Josephine Glapion. It is an interesting coincidence that this lady, who was related by marriage to the "other branch" of the Glapion family, reported Bertha Alcindor's death. She lived one block from Mrs. Alcindor at 2414 St. Philip Street and was probably her friend and fellow congregant at the nearby St. Peter Claver Church.[117] Josephine Glapion may have known Blair, Rose, or Cyril Legendre when they were still living in New Orleans. There is, however, no evidence that she held the official title of ownership to the Widow Paris tomb or had authority to open the vault for the placement of Bertha Alcindor's remains in 1957. The Carr-Llopis Mortuary lost the records of the Alcindor funeral and interment in a fire, so that possible source of information is now unavailable.[118]

ANALYSIS

Eighty-four people reside in the Widow Paris tomb, thirteen in the tomb on the St. Louis aisle, and thirteen in the vault in the Basin Street wall, making a total of 110. Analysis shows that seventy-six were persons of color and thirty-four were white. The black/white ratio was nearly equal during Marie's lifetime because she had friends, neighbors, clients, patients, and followers of all colors and classes, but later on most interments were of African Americans. Of those for whom the place of birth is certain, sixty-six were born in Louisiana (usually New Orleans); nine were immigrants from France, Italy, Ireland, Mexico, Cuba, and Haiti; and three were from elsewhere in the United States. Forty-six of the total burials were babies and toddlers (including many infants who were stillborn or died within the first months of life), nine were children ages two to thirteen years, thirty-five were women or adolescent girls, and twenty were men or adolescent boys.

The Burial Books and civil death certificates provide interesting data on the diseases and mishaps from which the people interred in Marie Laveau's three burial sites expired during the nineteenth and early twentieth centuries. Some babies died from "infant debility" or "maramus infantus," catch-all terms meaning that the little one simply was not strong enough to maintain a grasp on life. One died from "dentition" (teething). Infants, toddlers and older children died from diphtheria, typhoid, scarlet fever, measles, bronchitis, pneumonia, colitis, convulsions, tetanus, intestinal inflamation, and other ailments. Two children died from burns and two drowned.

Many adult deaths were caused by respiratory ailments: sixteen from tuberculosis (called "phthisis pulmonalis" or "consumption"), three from pneumonia, two from bronchitis, two from "abscess of the lungs," and one from asthma. Adults also died from various "pernicious" fevers and from maladies including heart disease, stroke (called "congestion of the brain" or "apoplexy"), intestinal infection (called "enteritis"), spinal meningitis, and nephritis. Some elderly people died from "senile debility" or "softening of the brain." One man died of alcoholism and one suffered a fatal gunshot wound. A nineteen-year-old youth drowned.

Marie Laveau was renowned for the nursing skills that she used to great effect during the city's cholera and yellow fever epidemics. She is said to have saved many lives, but one would still expect to find a number of victims of these diseases within the three burial sites of which she had use. Nobody who died from cholera or yellow fever was interred in the St. Louis aisle tomb or the Basin Street wall vault. The interment records for the Widow Paris tomb show only one woman and four children (one of them a baby great-granddaughter and one an unrelated boy who died at 152 St. Ann) who succumbed to cholera between 1866 and 1897. Dominique Moreau, a neighbor of the Laveau-Glapion family, died of yellow fever on September 16, 1870. There was a terrible yellow fever epidemic in 1878, and the civil death records and Archdiocesan Burial Books for that summer and fall are full of people who fell victim to the disease. Surprisingly, only two children, who both died of yellow fever on September 11, 1878, were placed in the Widow Paris tomb.[119] Maybe Marie indeed nursed many sufferers, but lost only these few.

I have identified the twenty-five family members, two slaves, eight friends, nine neighbors, and seven rentals interred in the Widow Paris tomb. Still, there are a total of fifty-nine people in the three burial sites who have no apparent connection to the Laveau-Glapion family. In many cases the entry in the Burial Book is the only record of their existence. They often had no civil death certificate, they did not turn up in city directories or the census, and there was no death or funeral announcement in the newspapers. Most of them lived and died in the mixed residential and industrial working-class Tremé neighborhood on St. Peter, Orleans, St. Ann, Dumaine, St. Philip, and Ursulines streets in the blocks between North Rampart Street and Claiborne Avenue and as far out toward Lake Pontchartrain as Galvez Street. They appear to have been nearly anonymous people inhabiting the fringes of New Orleans society.

They might have been babies that Marie helped to deliver, patients that she nursed in their last illness, clients, members of her Voudou congregation, or simply recipients of her charity. During this time when embalming was not customary, families faced with the death of a loved one, especially a sudden death for which they were unprepared, often had no tomb available for their use. Marie Laveau was known during her lifetime as a kind and charitable women, and these traits are reflected in her willingness to offer a final shelter to those who had no other burial place. Her daughter Philomène and grandson Blair Legendre carried on this tradition after Marie died in 1881. These family members indeed followed the obligation for devoted Catholics to "bury the dead," as stated in the Corporal Works of Mercy.

WHO OWNS THE
WIDOW PARIS TOMB?

It has been decades since any of the Laveau-Glapion descendants took any interest in maintaining the Widow Paris tomb or the other two burial sites in St. Louis Cemetery No. 1. They are what the Archdiocesan Cemeteries Office terms "orphaned" tombs. There is no public interest in the two-vault tomb on the St. Louis aisle or the Basin Street wall vault, and even the exact location of these sites is uncertain. The Widow Paris tomb, on the other hand, is a major tourist attraction and the focus of attention that is often destructive. Questions have arisen regarding who owns this tomb, who is responsible for its cleaning and repair, who has the right to be interred there, and whether it could be sold to a new owner who would use and care for it.

Ownership and the right to interment is complicated by the 1925 duplicate title in which the Archdiocese named Archange Glapion as proprietor of the tomb. At present, those who request information from the Archdiocesan Cemeteries Office are told only that it belongs to "the heirs of Archange Glapion." When pressed, the director of the Cemeteries Office explained to me that "heirship follows Louisiana law," meaning that if the owner of the tomb had no children, as is the case with Archange Glapion, heirship devolved to parents or siblings.[120] Only Archange's sister Philomène Glapion Legendre had direct surviving descendants, so these would be the official heirs. According to the Cemeteries Office, the representatives of a deceased person desiring to be interred in the Widow Paris tomb would need to produce the title of ownership or offer proof that the deceased is descended from Archange Glapion through the Glapion-Legendre line.

There have also been inquiries as to whether, since the Widow Paris tomb is considered "orphaned," a person unrelated to the family could buy and care for it. The director of the Cemeteries

Office explained that before the tomb could be sold, the potential buyer would have to provide "proper documentation listing all heirs to the tomb, and then all heirs must sign away their interest" to that buyer.[121]

In the early twentieth century, descendants of the Laveau-Glapion-Legendre line named Legendre and Karl were living in New Orleans and on the Mississippi Gulf Coast; descendants named Westenberg and Schmidt were living in St. Louis, Missouri; and descendants named Legendre, Santenac, and Baize were living in Louisville, Kentucky. A few of them continued to identify as African American, but most blended into the white community. By now there could be hundreds of descendants, with any number of surnames, and they might be living anywhere in the world. Sensationalistic twentieth-century writers portrayed Marie Laveau as a terrifying, witch-like figure, and her descendants, regardless of racial identity, might have been reluctant to claim the great Voudou priestess as their ancestor. Given families' tendency to keep such information secret, it is entirely possible that later generations are not even aware of their unique heritage. Given the uncertain identity, scattered location, and number of heirs, the requirement to locate and have them sign away their interest in the tomb seems like an impossible task.

CONCLUSION

A t the time of this writing, Spring 2016, the future of St. Louis Cemetery No. 1, and the Widow Paris tomb in particular, is difficult to predict. The strict rules enacted by the Archdiocese of New Orleans on March 1, 2015, were necessary to protect this historic cemetery from the depredations of careless tourists. On the other hand, the curtailment of free access to the Widow Paris tomb leaves bereft the Laveau devotees who consider her tomb a shrine and pilgrimage site. As of now, only tour groups (and the occasional lucky researcher) visit Marie Laveau's resting place. The tomb is white, pristine, unmarked, and devoid of offerings–a beloved queen stripped of her regalia.

As an alternative, Voudou priestess Sallie Ann Glassman created the International Shrine of Marie Laveau outside her Botánica Island of Salvation at the New Orleans Healing Center on St. Claude Avenue. The dedication ceremony was held on March 14, 2015. Although not the same as visiting the tomb in St. Louis Cemetery No. 1, this does provide a place for people who want to leave offerings and perform rituals.

At some point, might it be possible for some rapprochement to be reached between the Archdiocese of New Orleans and the larger community? Could visitors to the cemetery be dissuaded from committing acts of vandalism by enhanced security and education? Could Laveau devotees learn to communicate with Marie without marking on her tomb? Could the Archdiocese recognize that Catholicism and Voudou are not incompatible, and give permission for members of the Voudou congregation to visit the tomb and perform their religious rituals? Only the passage of time will answer these questions.

fig. 22: After St. Louis Cemetery No. 1 was closed to unaccompanied visitors, denying many devotees access to the Widow Paris tomb, Voudou priestess Sallie created the International Shrine of Marie Laveau at the New Orleans Healing Center. Photo by Carolyn Long at the dedication ceremony, March 14, 2015.

NOTES

1. Samuel Wilson Jr. and Leonard Huber, *The St. Louis Cemeteries of New Orleans* (New Orleans: Archdiocese of New Orleans, 1962). Leonard V. Huber, *"New Orleans Cemeteries: A Brief History,"* in *New Orleans Architecture, Volume III, The Cemeteries,* Mary Louise Christovich, ed. (Gretna, Louisiana: Pelican, 1974). Robert Florence (text) and Mason Florence (photographs), *New Orleans Cemeteries: Life in the Cities of the Dead* (New Orleans: Batture Press, 1997).

2. Wilson and Huber, *The St. Louis Cemeteries of New Orleans,* 49. In the key to the self-guided tour, the Widow Paris tomb is designated No. 3, "Glapion tomb, Alley No. 2-L, tomb No. 7, facing St. Louis Street," and the text of the bronze plaque is repeated.

3. For a complete history of Marie Laveau, see Carolyn Morrow Long, *A New Orleans Voudou Priestess: The Legend and Reality of Marie Laveau* (Gainesville: University Press of Florida, 2006). For a shorter history, see Carolyn Morrow Long, "Marie Laveau (1801-1881): A New Orleans Voudou Priestess," in Janet Allured and Judith Gentry, eds., *Louisiana Women, Their Lives and Times* (Athens: University of Georgia Press, 2009).

4. Descriptions of small, private ceremonies at the home of Marie Laveau come from Louisiana Writers' Project interviews, Cammie G. Henry Research Center, Federal Writers' Collection, Watson Memorial Library, Northwestern State University of Louisiana at Natchitoches (hereafter LWP). Marie Dédé, interview by Robert McKinney, n.d.; Raymond Rivaros, interview by Hazel Breaux, n.d.; Charles Raphael, interview by Hazel Breaux and Jacques Villere, n.d.; Oscar Felix, interview by Edmund Burke, March 14, 1940, LWP folder 25. Also see Long, *Voudou Priestess,* 93-118.

5. Laura Hopkins, interview by Maude Wallace February 9, 16, and 21, and March 4, 1940, and by Wallace and Henriette Michinard, April, 1940, LWP folder 43; Joe Landry, interview by Zoe Posey, July 18, 1939; John Slater, interview by Cecile Wright, n.d., LWP folder 25. "The Dead Voudou Queen," *New York Times,* June 23, 1881.

6. Descriptions of St. John's Eve celebrations come from LWP interviews with Oscar Felix; Charles Raphael; William Moore, interview by Edmund Burke, March 1, 1940; James Santana, interview by Zoe Posey, July 10, 1939; Joseph Alfred and Eugene Fritz, interview by Robert McKinney, n.d.; "Pops," interview by Robert McKinney, n.d., LWP folder 25. Newspaper stories include "The Voudous' Day," *New Orleans Times*, June 25, 1870; "The Vous Dous Incantation," *New Orleans Times*, June 28, 1872; "Voudou Vagaries—The Worshipers of Obeah Turned Loose," *New Orleans Times*, June 26, 1874; "Fetish Worship—St. John's Eve at Milneburg--A Voudou's Incantation--Midnight Scenes and Orgies," *New Orleans Times*, June 25, 1875; "St. John's Eve—After the Voudous--Some Singular Ceremonies—A Night in Heathenness," *New Orleans Daily Picayune*, June 25, 1875. See also Long, *Voudou Priestess*, 119-136.

7. "Voodooism," *New Orleans Commercial Bulletin*, July 5, 1869.

8. "The Voudous' Day," *New Orleans Times*, June 25, 1870. "The Vous Dous Incantation," *New Orleans Times*, June 28, 1872.

9. Robert Farris Thompson, *Flash of the Spirit: African and Afro-American Art and Philosophy* (New York: Vintage Books, 1983), 108-15.

10. Doris Kent, "Strange Old Wishing Vault in St. Louis Cemetery No. 2," *New Orleans Times-Picayune*, February 6, 1921. "Honor Voodoo Queen," *New Orleans Morning Tribune*, November 2, 1928. "Queen of Voodoo Rites Has Many Followers After Her Death," *New Orleans Times-Picayune*, February 8, 1934. "Voodoo Crosses Found on Grave of Noted Queen," *Baton Rouge Advocate*, June 22, 1936. Harry G. Head, "Cities Within a City–Down the Lanes of Memory Where the Dead Live On," *New Orleans Times-Picayune*, February 25, 1938.

11. Cruz Ayala, sexton of St. Louis Cemetery No. 1, interviewed by Maude Wallace, March 15, 1940 and by Hazel Breaux and Jacques Villere, n.d., attached to Rose Legendre interview, LWP folder 25. Cruz Ayala is listed in the New Orleans city directories from the late 1920s through the 1940s as a laborer for the St. Louis Cemeteries.

12. Lynne Jensen, "Voodon't—X Used to Mark the Spot" of Marie Laveau's Tomb, but Some Local Groups Hope to Lay the Practice to Rest," *New Orleans Times-Picayune,* May 27, 2005. The groups objecting to the practice were the Tour Guides Association of Greater New Orleans, the New Orleans Police Department, Save Our Cemeteries, and the Archdiocesan Cemeteries Office.

13. The pink paint was first discovered by Dorothy Morrison. Vanessa Bolano, "Marie Laveau Tomb Restored Just in Time for Halloween," October 30, 2014, WNGO News, *wgno.com/2014/10/30/marie-laveaus-resting-place-restoration-efforts-halloween-and-history.*

14. Richard A. Webster, "Ashes to Dust–Crumbling Historic St. Louis No. 1 Is Further Threatened by Unlicenced Guides", *New Orleans Times-Picayune,* April 27, 2014.

15. See *nolacatholiccemeteries.org/tourism/* and *clarionherald. info/clarion/index.php/archbishop-aymond/4161-finding-a-way-to-protect-st-louis-cemetery-no-1.* Copy of agreement between tour companies and the Archdiocesan Cemeteries Office provided by Mary Millan, Voudou priestess and director of Bloody Mary's Tours.

16. Susan Langenhennig, "Because of Vandalism, Only Tours Will Be Allowed in St. Louis No. 1 Cemetery," *www.nola.com/homegarden/ index.ssf/2015/01/because_of_vandalism_only_tour.html,* January 26, 2015.

17. Bennet Dowler, in "The Necropolis of New Orleans," *Medical and Surgical Journal* (November 1850), p. 279, wrote that the tombs are "private property, purchased under a written title or conveyance." Sales of cemetery lots and tombs by the Archdiocese were not typically enacted before a notary and will not be found in the Notarial Archives. Modern duplicate titles are issued by the Congregation of the St. Louis Cathedral and signed by the rector of the Cathedral.

18. Digital image of page from ledger book containing titles E-1 through E-183 provided by Sherri Peppo, director of the Archdiocesan Cemeteries Office; photocopy of ownership card for the "Archange Glapion tomb" provided by Alana Menzona, superintendent of St. Louis Cemeteries Office.

19. Michelle Stannard, owner of Bayou Preservation LLC, e-mail December 4, 2015.

20. Succession of Catherine Henry, June 28, 1831, Orleans Parish, Court of Probate, Probate and Succession Records: 1805-1848, 107 H 1831-1832, vol. 4, p. 317, City Archives, Louisiana Division, New Orleans Public Library

21. Bennet Dowler, "The Necropolis of New Orleans," *Medical and Surgical Journal,* November 1850, 275-300.

22. Wilson and Huber, *The St. Louis Cemeteries of New Orleans,* 18.

23. Funeral of Caroline Laveau Glapion, December 9, 1829, vol. 9, part 1, p. 2, act 8; funeral of Christophe (no surname), May 21, 1831, vol. 9, part 1, p. 129, act 848; funeral of Jean Baptiste Paris, July 12, 1832, vol. 9, part 2, p. 274, act 1730; funeral of François Glapion, May 18, 1834, vol. 10, part 3, p. 301, act 2019, all from St. Louis Cathedral/ Slaves and Free Persons of Color (hereafter SLC/S-FPC), Office of Archives and Records, Archdiocese of New Orleans (hereafter ARNO).

24. The tomb on the St. Louis aisle contained the bodies of Odille Bedenke, September 17, 1863, Burial Book 1859-1864, p. 204; Adele Chaperon, May16, 1864, Burial Book 1859-1864, p. 240; Elicia (no surname), May 24, 1864, Burial Book 1859-1864, p. 242; François Auguste, October 3, 1864, Burial Book 1859-1864, p. 273; Victoria Constant, September 7,1865, Burial Book 1865-1869, p. 127; Gaston D'Antry, March 4, 1869, Burial Book 1865-1869, p. 347; Andrew Sabbgast, September 19, 1873, Burial Book 1870-1873, p. 339; Gustave Buck, January 24, 1874, Burial Book 1874-1881, p. 57; Wallace Boucher, March 10, 1876, Burial Book 1874-1881, p. 164; Eugène Joseph Lajoie, May 10, 1881, Burial Book 1881-1883, p. 458; Fortuné Perrigore, June 22, 1883, Burial Book 1883-1886, p. 36; Rosalie Barron, September 19, 1883, Burial Book 1883-1886, p. 128; Annie Forber, February 28, 1886, Burial Book 1886-1892, p. 3. All ARNO.

25. The Basin Street wall vault contained the bodies of Louisa Peise, December 5, 1865, Burial Book 1870-1873, p. 274; Papite Micou, March 12, 1876, Burial Book 1874-1881, p. 164; Demasthenes Tapo, May 10, 1884, Burial Book 1883-1886, p. 99; Pradou Ouerto, August 11, 1885, Burial Book 1883-1886, p. 184; Son of Antoine Edward and Maria Monte, May 28, 1886, Burial Book 1886-1892, p. 64; Willie Martin, November 3, 1888, Burial Book 1886-1892, p. 125; Josephine Quinn, June 26, 1889, Burial Book 1886-1892, p. 156; Mrs. Allan Smith, June 27, 1890, Burial Book 1886-1892, p. 198; Antonio Jaffa, August 23, 1895, Burial Book 1893-1900, p. 120; Louise Baptist, January 26, 1901, Burial Book 1900-1912, part 1 , p. 69; Gustave Anderson, July 17, 1903, Burial Book 1900-1912, part 1, p. 162; George Capla, December 17, 1910, Burial Book 1900-1912, part 3, p. 428. All ARNO.

26. "Death of Marie Laveau—A Woman with a Wonderful History, Almost a Century Old, Carried to the Tomb Thursday Morning," *New Orleans Daily Picayune,* June 17, 1881. "Wayside Notes—The Death of Marie Laveau," *New Orleans City Item,* June 17, 1881. "Recollections of a Visit on New Years' Eve to Marie Laveau, the Ex-Queen of the Voudous," *New Orleans Daily States,* June 17, 1881. "The Dead Voudou Queen," *New York Times,* June 23, 1881. Less favorable comments about Marie Laveau were published in New Orleans' conservative newspapers: "Marie Lavaux—Death of the Queen of the Voudous Just Before St. John's Eve," *New Orleans Democrat,* June 17, 1881. "A Sainted Woman," *New Orleans Democrat,* June 18, 1881. "Voudou Vagaries—The Spirit of Marie Laveau to be Propitiated by Midnight Orgies on the Bayou," *New Orleans Times,* June 23, 1881.

27. "Death of Marie Laveau," *New Orleans Daily Picayune,* June 17, 1881, p. 8, c. 3.

28. Civil death certificate for Dame Christophe Glapion (Marie Laveau), June 15, 1881, vol. 78, p. 1113, Louisiana Department of Archives (hereafter LDA); interment June 16, 1881, Burial Book 1881-1883, p. 467 (the 1881-1883 records are included in the Burial Book for June-August 1873), ARNO. Shortly after the incident of the pink paint, Cemeteries Office director Sherri Peppo was quoted in the *Clarion Herald,* official newspaper of the Archdiocese, as saying that "As far as Marie Laveau being buried in the tomb, we do not have this in our records" (Christine Bordelon, "Vandals' Pink Paint Damage Removed at Laveau Tomb," *Clarion Herald*, January 14, 2014).

29. Interview with Tracy Dillon, Archdiocesan Cemeteries Office, April 2, 2014.

30. Alana Mendoza, superintendent of St. Louis Cemeteries Office, telephone interview February 17, 2000. This wall vault is officially designated as "Square Three, St. James Aisle, row twenty-five, range three." According to Ms. Mendoza, the wall was originally four vaults high, but the bottom one has sunk. The top vault is in range 4, the middle one is range 3, the bottom is range 2, and range 1 is now below ground. Range 4, the top vault, belonged to the Desdunes family.

31. Civil death certificate for Christophe Glapion, June 26, 1855, vol. 17, p. 42, LDA; Funeral announcement, *New Orleans Bee*, June 27, 1855, p. 2, c. 5. Christophe Duminy de Glapion, Interment Payment Records St. Louis Cemetery No. 1, June 27, 1855, vol. 5, part 1, p. 263, No. 737, ARNO.

32. See Long, *Voudou Priestess*, 79-85, for a full account of the financial crisis suffered by the Laveau-Glapion family around the time of Christophe Glapion's death.

33. Baptism of Archange Edouard (no surname), SLC/ S-FPC, May 7, 1839, unnumbered volume for 1838, act 438, ARNO; civil death certificate for Archange Glapion, January 5, 1838, vol. 10, p. 297, LDA.

34. Baptism of Marie Heloïse Glapion, SLC/S-FPC, August 19, 1828, vol. 21, p. 220, act 1232 (the baptism was not entered in the register until February, 1829), ARNO.

35. Robert Tallant, *Voodoo in New Orleans* (1946, reprint Gretna, La.: Pelican, 1983). Tallant's book is based on interviews conducted by the Louisiana Writers' Project and crafted into a 700-page "Voodoo" manuscript by Project employee Catherine Dillon, LW P folders 118, 317, and 319. Dillon and Tallant both specify February 2, 1827, as the birth date of "Marie II." Earlier works also cite this date: Lyle Saxon, *Fabulous New Orleans* (1928, reprint Gretna, La.: Pelican, 1988), 243; Zora Neale Hurston, "Hoodoo in America," *Journal of American Folklore* 44, No. 174 (1931), 315-316; *Mules and Men* (1935, reprint New York: Harper Perennial Library, 1990), 191-95. For more on the alleged "Marie II," see Long, *Voudou Priestess,* 191-205.

36. "Victor Pierre Crocker, who resides in this city and is of the full age of majority, respectfully represents that his mother, the late Eloise Euchariste Glapion...departed this life in this city in the month of June, 1862; that she died intestate; that she has left neither lawful children or descendants or legitimate collateral heirs; that she has left as her sole and only issue her natural son, the petitioner, who has been always acknowledged by her as such.... Petitioner prays to be put in possession of...a lot of ground and buildings thereon in the Third District of this city, Faubourg Marigny, forming part of lot No. 207, in the square bounded by Love (Rampart), Craps (Burgundy), Union (Pauger), and Bagatelle (Truro) Streets." Testimony of Victor Pierre Crocker, Succession of Eloise Euchariste Glapion, Judgement No. 4597, Civil District Court, NOPL. This property is now 1930 North Rampart Street.

37. Madame Widow Oscar *née* Glapion, July 20, 1860, Burial Book 1859-1864, p. 103, ARNO.

38. Baptism of Joseph Eugène Crocker, St. Augustine's Church S-FPC, May 18, 1844, vol. 1A, act 13, p. 19, ARNO.

39. U.S. Census for New Orleans 1850, Widow Paris, sheet 178, line 3-7; U. S. Census for New Orleans 1860, Widow Paris, ward 5, sheet 649, line 24-28; U. S. Census for New Orleans 1870, Mary Paris, sheet 78, line 14-18, accessed through Ancestry.com. Adelai Aldina, Onesta, and Victor Pierre Crocker are listed under various names in the 1850, 1860, and 1870 census.

40. Baptism of Adelai Glapion, SLC/ S-FPC February 3, 1848, vol. 32, Part 2, p. 353, ARNO.

41. Civil death certificate for Aldina Croker, September 9, 1871, vol. 52, p. 245, LDA. Interment of A. Aldina Croker, September 10, 1871, Burial Book 1870-1873, p. 215, ARNO.

42. Baptism of Marie Glapious (Onesta Crocker), July 9, 1850, SLC/ S-FPC, vol. 32, part 3, p. 454, ARNO. U. S. Census for New Orleans 1850, Widow Paris, sheet 178, line 3-7; U. S. Census for New Orleans 1860, Widow Paris, ward 5, sheet 649, line 24-28, accessed through Ancestry.com.

43. Civil marriage certificate for Alexis Glapion and Marie Marguerite Mansini, April 17, 1868, vol. 678, p. 98, LDA. Marriage of Alexis C. Glapion and Marie Marguerite Onesta Crocker, SLC/S-FPC, vol. 5, p. 7, act 32, ARNO, cited in Barbara Trevigne, "Ball of Confusion: Célestin Glapion and the Glapion Family of Louisiana," *New Orleans Genesis* (October 2010), 314, 331, n. 49 and 51.

44. U.S. Census for New Orleans 1870, Mary Paris, Célestin "Glapillon," painter, and wife Honesta, sheet 78, line 14-18, accessed through Ancestry.com.

45. The ownership of Lizette and her children Célestin and Marie by Jean Baptiste de Glapion, his paternity of the children, and the subsequent emancipation of Lizette, Célestin, and Marie is detailed in Barbara Trevigne's article "Ball of Confusion," 306-08.

46. Barbara Trevigne describes two fine armoires, now at the Louisiana State Museum and the Historic New Orleans Collection, believed to have been made by the first Célestin Glapion (Trevigne, "Ball of Confusion," 310-14). Célestin's son Célestin Pierre was a carpenter and his grandson Alexis Célestin was a house painter.

47. Civil death certificate for Henry Raphael Glapion, September 15, 1873, death reported by D. (Derozin) Gondron, vol. 59, p. 356, LDA; interment Burial Book 1870-1873, p. 339, ARNO. Civil death certificate for Antoine Raphael, October 17, 1874, death reported by (Alexandre) Glapion Legendre, vol. 62, p. 136, LDA; interment Burial Book, 1874-1881, p. 88, ARNO.

48. Civil death certificate for Onesta Oscar Mansini, November 22, 1846, death reported by her husband Célestin Glapion, vol. 67, p. 613, LDA; interment November 23, 1876, Burial Book 1874-1881, p. 211, ARNO. Onesta's name was incorrectly entered into the Burial Book as "Célestine Glapion," and her age was incorrectly given as twenty-three.

49. Civil marriage certificate for Alexis Célestin Glapion and Emma Vicknaire, May 26, 1877, vol. 6, p. 266, LDA. For his children with Perez and Valentine, see Trevigne, "Ball of Confusion," note 53, p. 332.

50. U.S. Census for New Orleans 1870, Mary Paris, "John Croquoir," barber, was a member of the household, sheet 78, line 14-18, accessed through Ancestry.com. City directory 1874, Pierre Crocker, barber; city directory1891, John Crocker, barber.

51. Civil marriage certificate for Victor Pierre Crocker and Catherine Teche, May 5, 1877, vol. 12, p. 512, LDA. Victor Pierre was stated to be the son of Perriquite (Pierre) Crocker and Anne H. D. (Heloïse Duminy?) Glapion. Marriage of Victor Pierre Crocker and Catherine Teche, Widow of Armand Massel, SLC, May 5, 1887, vol. 16, p. 193, ARNO (note that after 1870 the church no longer kept separate books for white persons and persons of color).

52. Civil death certificate for John Croker (Victor Pierre Crocker), August 14, 1892, death reported by his cousin, Alex Legendre, vol. 102, p. 551, LDA; interment Burial Book 1886-1892, p. 300, ARNO. U.S. Census for New Orleans 1900, Enumeration District 67, Ward 7, Catherine Croquor, widow, living with her mother Pauline Teche, sheet 16B, line 66, accessed through Ancestry.com.

53. Civil birth certificate for Philomène Glapion, June 1, 1836, vol. 4, p. 159, LDA. Baptism of Phélonise Lavan, SLC/ S-FPC, April 1, 1836, vol. 25, act 100, p. 35; corrected baptism of Philomène Glapion, May 31, 1836, act 363, unnumbered volume for 1838, SLC/S-FPC, ARNO.

54. Judith Legendre enrolled her children in private schools after arriving in New York City: U.S. Census for New York City 1850,

Ward 18, Amanda Legendre, student at Madame Chegary's school, 113B, line 3. U. S. Census for West Farms, Westchester, New York 1850, Gustave and Arthur Legendre, students at Roman Catholic College, sheet 288, line 3 and 4. U. S. Census for New York City 1860, Judith Legendre, Arthur Legendre, and Gustave Legendre, Ward 18, District 2, sheet 267, line 16-18. All accessed through Ancestry.com.

55. Baptism of Eugènie Glapion, St. Augustine's Church/ S-FPC, vol. 3, p. 206, ARNO. Civil death certificate for Eugènie Legendre, January 29, 1866, vol. 32, p. 289, LDA; interment January 30,1866, Burial Book 1865-1869, p. 146, ARNO. Civil birth certificates for Charles St. Marc and Etienne St. Marc Legendre, twins, February 10, 1870, vol. 53, p. 289; civil death certificate for Charles Legendre, February 11, 1870, vol. 47, p. 897; Joseph Legendre, May 24, 1870, vol. 52, p. 245, LDA; interment for Joseph Legendre, February 12, 1870; Charles Legendre, May 24,1870, Burial Book 1870-1873, p. p. 111 and 127, ARNO.

56. Civil death certificate for Emile Alexandre Legendre, July 26, 1872, vol. 55, p. 263, LDA; interment St. Louis Cemetery No. 3, section B, St. Joseph alley, Louisiana Writers' Project cemetery files.

57. Deposition of Marie Laveau taken by John Cain, Fourth Justice of the Peace for Orleans Parish, on February 24, 1873, at 153 St. Ann as evidence in the Second District Court in the Succession of Pierre Monette, Louisiana Wills and Probate Records, accessed through Ancestry.com. (Thanks to Jennifer Morris for alerting me to this source.)

58. U.S. Census for New Orleans 1880, Marie Glapion, Philomène Legendre, Fidelia Legendre, Noëmie Legendre, Alexander Legendre, Enumeration District 35, sheet 38B, line 45, accessed through Ancestry.com. The 1890 census was destroyed by fire, and by 1900 the family had dispersed.

59. "Flagitious Fiction: Cable's Romance About Marie Laveau and the Voudous," *New Orleans Daily Picayune,* April 11, 1886. "Voudooism-A Chapter of Old New Orleans History," *New Orleans Daily Picayune,* June 22, 1890.

60. Civil birth certificate for "Tidelia" (Fidelia) Alexandre Legendre, November 17, 1857, vol. 49, 746, LDA.

61. Marriage of Fidelia Legendre and Julius Westenberg, SLC, November 17, 1890, vol. 16, p. 589, ARNO. U. S. Census for St. Louis 1910, Ward 13, ED 218, family of Julius Westenberg, sheet 20A, lines 7-11; U. S. Census for St. Louis 1920, Ward 13, ED 270, sheet 22A, line 20; U. S. Census for St. Louis 1930, ED 96-495, sheet 6A, line 8-11, accessed through Ancestry.com.

62. Civil birth certificate for Noëmie Marguerite Legendre, October 10, 1862, vol. 49, p. 746, LDA.

63. Civil marriage certificate for Noëmie Legendre and Joseph [sic] Santenac, October 16, 1880, vol. 13, p. 155, LDA; marriage of Noëmie Marguerite Legendre and John Benjamin Santenac, October 16, 1880, SLC, vol. 15, p. 87, ARNO. Information on the race of Benjamin Santenac's family comes from U.S. Census for New Orleans 1870, Ward 5, sheet 119, line 20, accessed through Ancestry. com, showing that his father, Joseph Santenac, was from France and his mother, Margaret Murray, was from Ireland. The whole family, including brothers Bernard, Louis, and Auguste, was classified as white.

64. Civil birth certificate for Benjamin Alexander Saintignac [sic], January 17, 1881, vol. 76, p. 965, LDA. There are no civil birth certificates for Antoinette and Marita.

65. "Drowned in a Canal," *New Orleans Daily Picayune*, September 17, 1894; "A Girl Drowned—Antoinette Santenac Meets her Death in the Orleans Canal," *New Orleans Item*, September 17, 1894. Interment of Antoinette Santenac, September 17, 1894, Burial Book 1893-1900, p. 77, ARNO.

66. Civil death certificate for Marita Santenac, December 7, 1894, vol. 107, p. 575, LDA; interment December 8, 1894, Burial Book 1893-1900, p. 85, ARNO.

67. Civil birth certificate for Alexandre Glapion Legendre, May 8, 1859, vol. 49, p. 746, LDA.

68. Marriage of Alexandre Legendre and Mathilde Lachapelle, June 24, 1885, SLC, vol. 15, p. 581, ARNO. Civil birth certificate for Blair Manuel Legendre, July 16, 1887, vol. 85, p. 666, LDA.

69. Civil birth certificate for Arthur Legendre, October 2, 1885, vol. 83, p. 328; Ernest Alexander Legendre, November 16, 1887, vol. 86, p. 326; Amalie Legendre, January 27, 1890, vol. 97, p. 100; Pierre Legendre, January 27, 1892, vol. 106, p. 578, Pauline Legendre, October 1, 1894, vol. 106, p. 578, LDA.

70. Civil death certificate for "Amelia" Legendre, April 3, 1896, vol. 110, p. 939, LDA.

71. Civil death certificate for Ernestine "Laddo," March 26, 1897, vol. 113, p. 474, LDA. Interment Burial Book 1893-1900, p. 180, ARNO.

72. Civil death certificate for Clara Westenberg, April 5, 1897, vol. 113, p. 549, LDA; interment Burial Book 1893-1900, p. 181, ARNO.

73. Civil death certificate for Mary (Marie) Legendre, April 16, 1897, vol. 113, p. 618, LDA; interment Burial Book 1893-1900, p. 182, ARNO. The baby died exactly 21 days after Ernestine Llado. Her parents names were not specified, but she was undoubtedly Ernestine and Alex's newborn child.

74. Civil death certificate for Philomène Legendre, June 11, 1897, vol. 114, p. 15, LDA; interment June 11, 1897, Burial Book 1893-1900, p. 189, ARNO.

75. Interment of Edouard Eastin, September 9, 1860, Burial Book 1859-1864, p. 48, ARNO.

76. This slab is designated as No. 2010, "fragment display" on the Dead Space map and survey database.

77. Interment of Jean Louis, January 9, 1835, Burial Book 1834-1835, p. 243, ARNO; interment of Marie, October 29, 1861, Burial Book 1859-1864, p. 119, ARNO.

78. Marie Laveau and Christophe Glapion's slave ownership is documented in Long, *Voudou Priestess,* 69-78.

79. Sale of slave Juliette by Pierre Monette to Marie Laveau, November 15, 1847, Acts of Paul Laresche, vol. 2, act 223, NARC. Sale of slave Eliza by Christophe Glapion to Pierre Monette, Acts of A. E. Bienvenu, April 26, 1854, vol. 5, act 62, NARC. Barbara Trevigne discovered that, as legal guardian to Marguerite Onesta Crocker, Pierre Monette granted permission for her to marry Alexis Célestin Glapion, "Ball of Confusion" p. 331, n. 49 and 51.

80. Civil death certificate for Pierre Monette, April 24, 1872, death reported by D. [Derozin] Gondron, 152 St. Ann, vol. 54, p. 303, LDA; interment April 25, 1872, Burial Book 1870-1873, p. 254, ARNO. Civil death certificate for Charles Albert Monette, son of Julien Joseph Monette, July 11, 1872, vol. 55, p. 170, LDA ; interment July12, 1872, Burial Book 1870-1873, p. 269. ARNO. Civil death certificate for Mme Edouard Monette, August 12, 1872, vol. 55, p. 359, LDA; interment Burial Book 1870-1873, p. 274, ARNO. Deposition of Marie Laveau in the Succession of Pierre Monette, Louisiana Wills and Probate Records, accessed through Ancestry.com.

81. Louise Hermance Monette, daughter of Julien Joseph Monette, had a relationship with Edward Joseph Lamothe resulting in the birth of a son, Ferdinand Joseph, later known as Jelly Roll Morton. The exact birth date of this child is unknown—most sources say 1890, but others say 1889, 1884 or 1885. Information from Ancestry.com and *www.doctorjazz.co.uk/genealogy.html.*

82. "Lucien Adams—His Historic Character Succumbs to a Paralytic Stroke," *New Orleans Daily Picayune,* March 2, 1900.

83. Tallant, *Voodoo in New Orleans,* 60, 105.

84. Marguerite Gitson, interview by Zoe Posey, February 20, 1941; Mary Washington, interview by Robert McKinney, n.d.; Nathan Hobley, interview by Zoe Posey, January, 1941, all from LWP folder 25.

85. *New Orleans Daily Picayune,* "A Bloody Fracas—Riot at a Southern Republican Club Meeting," April 6, 1876, p. 1; "Death of Lucien Adams Jr., Expired at 10 o'clock this Morning," April 7, p. 2; "Mechanics Institute–The Riot Last Night, Coroner Chantant's Investigation," April 9, p. 4.

86. Interment of Lucien Adams Jr., April 7, 1876, Burial Book 1874-1881, p. 168, ARNO.

87. Civil death certificate for Virginia Bienvenu (Fagot), May 6, 1881, vol. 78, p. 717, LDA; interment May 7, 1881, Burial Book 1881-1883, p. 458, ARNO.

88. Charles Raphael, interview by Hazel Breaux and Jacques Villere, n.d., Louisiana Writers' Project folder 25. Mr. Raphael stated that "The Marie Laveau tomb in St. Louis Cemetery No. 1 had originally belonged to the Lionel Adams family, and that he was not sure how Marie came into possession of it, but that after Marie's death, Adams' sister was in the habit of visiting the grave regularly." Lionel Adams, a deputy clerk of the Criminal Court, was one of five sons of Judge Lucien Adams. Lionel's sisters were Constance and Louisiana.

89. E-mail correspondence with Adams family descendants Leslie Adams and Ann Hargrave Knight, October 2014 - May 2016. Leslie Adams provided a digital image of a duplicate title to the Adams family tomb in St. Louis Cemetery No. 1, No. 9, alley 2 right facing Basin Street, owner Lucien Adams Sr., original sale 1819, issued February 11, 1953.

90. Sale by State of Louisiana of property belonging to Marie Philomène Glapion for unpaid taxes to Fidelia Legendre represented by Lucien Adams, Acts of Alphonse Rabouin, December 31, 1886, vol. 1, p. 229, NARC.

91. Civil death certificate for Manuel Legendre, May 9, 1876, death reported by G. Wiltz, 210 Bourbon Street (a man named Rodolph Wiltz, clerk, was listed at 152 St. Ann in the 1878 city directory), vol. 66, p. 127, LDA. Interment May 10, 1876, Burial Book 1874-1881, p. 174, ARNO.

92. Civil death certificate for Charles Ernest Llado, June 12, 1887, vol. 91, p. 402 LDA; interment June 13, 1887, Burial Book 1886-1892, p. 65, ARNO. Joseph Yado [Llado], interment April 8, 1910, Burial Book 1900-1912 book 3, p. 406. Delphine Llado, interment January 22, 1885, Burial Book 1883-1886, p. 151, ARNO.

93. The system of house numbering used during most of the nineteenth century changed in 1894, meaning that pre-1894 addresses are not usable in the present day. To determine exactly where an individual lived and died, I turned to the 1883 Robinson's Atlas and the 1885 and 1886 Sanborn Maps of New Orleans to find these dwellings. Locating the addresses of those who died after 1894 presented no problem.

94. Antoine Cuney, interment June 1, 1869, Burial Book 1865-1869, p. 361. Pauline Vigne, civil death certificate, death reported by A. [Alex] Legendre residing at 152 St. Ann Street, February 24, 1892, vol. 101, p. 329, LDA; interment February 24, 1892, Burial Book 1886-1892, p. 274. Albert Becknou, interment September 5, 1894, Burial Book 1893-1900, p. 76. All ARNO.

95. Dominique Moreau, civil death certificate September 16, 1870, vol. 48, p. 530, LDA; interment September 17, 1870, Burial Book 1870-1873, p. 151. Corine Ayala, interment June 22, 1874, Burial Book 1874-1881, p. 73. John Eaton, interment January 6, 1877, Burial Book 1874-1881, p. 219. Leliha Fegue, interment April 20, 1878, Burial Book 1874-1881, p. 285. Lucie Billard, interment August 8, 1880, Burial Book 1874-1881, p. 317. Joseph Alexander McLean, interment March 1, 1889, Burial Book 1886-1892, p. 141. Etienne Felix, civil death certificate October 11, 1870, vol. 48, p. 760; LDA; interment Burial Book 1870-1873, p. 158. All ARNO.

96. Caroline Julien, interment February 25, 1872, Burial Book 1870-1873, p. 247. Ida Durand, civil death certificate August 20, 1873, vol. 59, p. 153, LDA; interment Burial Book 1870-1873, p. 334. Henriette Lamayer, civil death certificate March 17, 1873, vol. 57, p. 451, LDA; interment Burial Book 1870-1873, p. 309. Felix Michael Gaudet, civil death certificate February 2, 1878, vol. 71, p. 557, LDA; interment Burial Book 1874-1881, p. 275. All ARNO.

97. Henry Gusman, interment May 31, 1878, Burial Book 1874-1881, p. 289. Angela Sapata, interment March 4, 1879, Burial Book 1874-1881, p. 352, ARNO.

98. Lucien Gex, civil death certificate May 31, 1876, vol. 66, p. 338, LDA; interment Burial Book 1874-1881, p. 180, ARNO.

99. Sale of lot with buildings for $1,000 by Noëmie Legendre, wife of Benjamin Santenac, to Clement Dabezies, Acts of Antoine Doriocourt, September 24, 1897, vol. 54, act 59, Notarial Archives Research Center.

100. Civil death certificate for Fidelia Westenberg, December 29, 1898, vol. 37, p. 155, St. Louis Bureau of Vital Statistics, Division of Health. U.S. Census for St. Louis 1910, Julius Westenberg remarried to Nannie Schwanneke, living with Nannie, her adult children, and his son Julius Jr., ED 218, sheet 20, line 6-11. U. S. Census for St. Louis 1920, Julius Westenberg living with Anna and Frank Schmidt and their son Frank, ED 270, sheet 22A, line 20-23. U. S. Census for St. Louis 1930, Julius Westenberg, Anna and Frank Schmidt, children Frank and Virginia Schmidt, ED 96-495, sheet 6A, line 8-12. All accessed through Ancestry.com.

101. U.S. Census for Louisville 1910, John Zoller and wife "Nemie," stepson Alexander Santenac, niece and nephew Pauline and Frank Legendre, Ward 11, Enumeration District 191, sheet 6A, lines 15-19. U. S. Census for Louisville 1920, John and Noëmie "Zaller," niece Pauline "Levy" (Legendre), grandson Emile Santenac, and grandniece Noëmie Baize, ED 21, sheet 6A, lines 35-39. U. S. Census for Louisville 1930, John and "Naomi" Zoller, niece Ogaletta Zoller, ED 119, sheet 59A, lines 39-41. U. S. Census for Louisville 1940, Frank P. and Katie Legendre, daughters Ernestine and Mary Catherine, ED 290, sheet 8A, lines 7-10. Civil birth certificate for Francis Ernest Legendre, son of Frank Legendre and Katherine Agnes Smith, Jefferson County, Kentucky, July 31, 1922, No. 39860. All accessed through Ancestry.com.

102. Civil death certificate for Noëmie M. Zoller, March 11, 1934, Kentucky Death Records, file 6588, register No. 1044; interment at

Calvary Cemetery, Louisville, Kentucky; accessed through Ancestry. com.

103. Civil death certificate for Alexander Legendre, January 7, 1903, vol. 128, p. 1184, LDA; interment January 8, 1903, Burial Book 1900-1912 book 1, p. 142 ARNO.

104. Civil birth certificate for Blair Manuel Legendre, July 16, 1887, vol. 85, p. 666, LDA. With his wife Carmen Madere, Blair Manuel had children Rodney (born July 27, 1920, died Los Angeles, California October 31, 1996), Mabel (born May 1, 1923, died New Orleans December 1976), and Leonard Blair (born May 1, 1924, died New Orleans January 7, 1992). Mabel Legendre is buried at Westlawn Memorial Park in Gretna, Louisiana. None of them had any known children. Manuel Legendre and family (all Negro), U.S. Census for New Orleans 1930, Ward 7, ED 36-116, sheet 1A, line 31-35; U.S. Census for New Orleans 1940, ED 36-154, sheet 3B, line 60-64, accessed through Ancestry.com.

105. U.S. Census for New Orleans 1910, Arthur Legendre (white), living in the household of his uncle Blair Legendre, Ward 6, ED 100, sheet 4B, line 5, accessed through Ancestry.com.

106. U.S. Census for New Orleans 1910, Ernest Legendre (white), living alone, Ward 7, ED 109, sheet 3A, line 4. Civil marriage certificate for Ernest Alexander Legendre and Violet Jeanne Caubert, April 30, 1910, vol. 32, p. 177, LDA. Ernest Legendre ("caucasian"), WWI draft registration 1917. U.S. Census for New Orleans 1920, Ernest Legendre and family (white), Ward 13, ED 222, sheet 11B, line 70-76; and U.S. Census for New Orleans 1930, ED 222, sheet 5B, line 89-93. U.S. Census for New Orleans 1940, Ernest Legendre and family (white), ED 1, sheet 6A, line 5; Ernest Legendre (white), WWII draft registration card 1942. All accessed through Ancestry.com. "Deaths," *New Orleans Times-Picayune* September 12, 1948; Ernest Legendre's funeral was held at Our Lady Star of the Sea Catholic Church and he was buried in Greenwood Cemetery.

107. Theodore Charles Legendre (born January 10, 1911, died 1978 New Orleans); Theodore was married to Gladys Bertoneire,

"Deaths," *New Orleans Times-Picayune,* December 26, 1978, buried in Cypress Grove Cemetery. Ethel Claire Legendre Karl (born May 4, 1912, died Bay St. Louis, Hancock County, Mississippi, February 18, 2005); Ethel was first married to William Biuro and then to William Karl; buried in Gulf Coast Memorial Cemetery. Thomas Ernest Legendre (born December 13, 1913, died Bay St. Louis, Hancock County, Mississippi, October 27, 1989); Thomas was married to Cecile Elizabeth Kellogg; buried in Gulf Coast Memorial Cemetery. U.S. Census for New Orleans 1940, Ethel (Legendre), her husband William Biuro, her mother Violet Legendre, and brother Thomas Legendre, ED 1, sheet 10A, line 2-5. U.S. Census for New Orleans 1940, Theodore Legendre and wife Gladys, ED 1, sheet 8A, line 32-33. Death Theodore Legendre, age 68, New Orleans, December 23, 1978, interment at Cypress Grove Cemetery, *New Orleans Times-Picayune,* p. 16, c. 5 ; Ethel C. Karl, age 92, Bay St. Louis, Mississippi, February 27, 2005; Thomas Legendre, age 76, Bay St. Louis, Mississippi, October 27, 1989, Social Security Death Index. Ethel and Thomas interred in Gulf Coast Memorial Cemetery, U.S. Find A Grave Index. All accessed through Ancestry.com.

108. Civil birth certificate for Blair Arthur Legendre, October 18, 1868, vol. 49, p. 147, LDA.

109. U.S. Census for New Orleans 1910, Blair Legendre and family, ward 6, ED 100, sheet 4A, line 48; U. S. Census for New Orleans 1920, ward 7, ED 125, sheet 12, line 2; U. S. Census for New Orleans 1930, ED 106, sheet 31B, line 99, accessed through Ancestry.com.

110. Cruz Ayala, sexton of St. Louis Cemetery No. 1, interview by Hazel Breaux and Jacques Villere, n.d. (probably 1940), LWP folder 25. Rose Legendre, interview by Maude Wallace, March 20, 1940, and by Hazel Breaux and Jacques Villere, n.d, folder 25, LWP.

111. U.S. Census for New Orleans 1940, Rose Legendre and son Cyril, 2716 Havana Street, Ward 7, sheet 61A, line 18. Cyril Legendre, WWII draft registration card 1942, all accessed through Ancestry.com. Cyril Legendre was listed at 2716 Havana on his draft registration and in the 1945 city directory.

112. Civil death certificate for Cyril John Legendre, October 18, 1965, file No. 65-122655, State of California Department of Health Services. Funeral arrangements by Spalding Mortuary, burial in Holy Cross Cemetery, Los Angeles.

113. Louise Baptist, interment January 26, 1901, Burial Book 1900-1912, part 1, p. 69. Gustave Anderson, interment July 17, 1903, Burial Book 1900-1912, part 1, p. 162. George Capla, interment December 18, 1910, Burial Book 1900-1912, part 3, p. 428. All ARNO.

114. Civil death certificate for Camille Quintelle [Kintell], March 10, 1904, vol. 132, p. 173, LDA; interment Burial Book 1900-1912, part 2, p. 188. Civil death certificate for Mary Mathieu, February 9, 1912, vol. 154, p. 240, LDA; interment Burial Book 1900-1912, part 3, p. 466; Civil death certificate for Julianne V. Philips, December 27, 1917, vol. 170, p. 1088, LDA; interment Burial Book 1913-1919, p. 262, opening ordered by Blair Legendre. All ARNO.

115. Bertha Alcindor, interment August 20, 1957, Burial Book 1921-1973, p. 242, ARNO. New Orleans city directory 1956, Bertha Alcindor, (no occupation), 2515 St. Philip. Bertha was the widow of Alexander Alcindor, who died in 1933.

116. Funeral notice for Bertha Alcindor, *New Orleans Times-Picayune,* August 19, 1957.

117. Civil death certificate for Bertha Alcindor, City of New Orleans file no. 57 5520, LDA. Thanks to Leila Bristow and Kathleen Wieland of the USGenWeb Orleans Parish genealogy listserv for helping to identify Josephine Glapion, *née* Grubbs, wife of Walter Andrew Glapion. New Orleans city directories from the 1950s list Walter and Josephine Glapion living at 2414 St Philip, one block from Bertha Alcindor. This was also near St. Peter Claver Church at 1922 St. Philip, where the Alcindor funeral was held. None of these addresses are near 2716 Havana Street, last known residence of Rose Legendre and her son Cyril. Walter Andrew Glapion, son of Peter (Pierre) and Edna Glapion, was baptized at St. Peter Claver Church on October 1, 1910, and confirmed there in June 1921, Barbara Trevigne, "Glapion

Genealogy: Ten Generations from Françoise Kernion," *New Orleans Genesis* (January 2011), p. 31, n. 174 and 176. Civil marriage certificate for Walter Andrew Glapion and Joseph [*sic*] Mary Grubbs, June 1930, vol. 52, p. 779, LDA.

118. Telephone interview, August 26, 2015, with Lambert Bossiere Jr., whose father brought Carr-Llopis Mortuary in 1955.

119. Cholera: Carmelite Feraud, interred August 8, 1866, Burial Book 1865-1869, p. 169; Felix Bertoulin, interred January 9, 1868, Burial Book 1865-1869, p. 287; Antoine Cuney (died at 152 St. Ann), interred June 1, 1869, Burial Book 1865-1869, p. 361; Justine, interred June 27, 1876, Burial Book 1874-1881, p. 186; Clara Westenberg (great-granddaughter), interred April 5, 1897, Burial Book 1893-1900, p. 181. Yellow fever: Dominique Moreau, interment September 17, 1870, Burial Book 1870-1873, p. 151; Lucie Billard and Henry Bertrand, both interred September 12, 1878, Burial Book 1874-1881, p. 317 and 318. All ARNO.

120. "Descent and Distribution of Property: If the father or mother of the person who has died without issue has died before him, the portion which would have been inherited by such deceased parent goes to the brothers and sisters of the deceased, or their descendants." Alcée Fortier, *Louisiana: Comprising Sketches of Counties, Towns, Events, Institutions, and Persons Arranged in Cyclopedic Form*, Vol. 1, 321-22 (Atlanta: Southern Historical Association, 1909).

121. E-mail correspondence with Sherri Peppo, Director of Archdiocesan Cemeteries Office, April 22, 2015, and August 26, 2015.

TOMB OF THE WIDOW PARIS BORN LAVEAU
ST. LOUIS CEMETERY NO. 1

RESEARCH IN THE FUNERAL AND BURIAL BOOKS
AT THE OFFICE OF ARCHIVES AND RECORDS
ARCHDIOCESE OF NEW ORLEANS

Possible interments in the Widow Paris tomb, from funeral records, Office of Archives and Records :

Marguerite Henry/Darcantel (mother of Marie Laveau), funeral July 31, 1825

Marie Louise Caroline Glapion (child of Marie Laveau and Christophe Glapion), funeral December 9, 1829

Christophe Glapion (child of Marie Laveau and Christophe Glapion), funeral May 21, 1831

Catherine Henry (grandmother of Marie Laveau), funeral June 18, 1831

Jean Baptiste Glapion (child of Marie Laveau and Christophe Glapion), funeral July 12, 1832

Relatives, family slaves, family friends, and any who died at 152 St. Ann Street are noted as FAMILY, SLAVE, FRIEND or NEIGHBOR. Each entry is designated BABY, CHILD, or ADULT, COLORED or WHITE. The location of the tomb is designated as WP for Widow Paris tomb without vault; if vault is given, as LOWER, MIDDLE, or UPPER. The numbers in parentheses indicate how many of each category.

Interments known from inscriptions on the tomb:

1.

FAMILY, CHILD (1)	COLORED	WP, MIDDLE (1)

Archange Glapion (son of Marie Laveau and Christophe Glapion), inscription middle vault and on tablet set into sidewalk, death certificate January 5, 1845

2.

FAMILY, CHILD (2)	COLORED	WP, MIDDLE (2)

Joseph Eugène Crocker (son of Eloise Glapion and Pierre Crocker, grandson of Marie and Christophe), 1849, inscription on middle vault and on tablet set into pavement

3.

FAMILY, CHILD (3)	COLORED	WP, MIDDLE (3)

Esmeralda Crocker (daughter of Eloise Glapion and Pierre Crocker, granddaughter of Marie and Christophe), 1850, inscription on middle vault

4.

FAMILY, CHILD (4)	COLORED	WP, NO VAULT (1)

Eugène Eastin (son of Edouard Eastin and Louise Pauline Gendron, grand-nephew of Marie and Christophe) born July 24, 1856, died September 6, 1857. A marble tablet with inscriptions for Eugène and his brother Edouard is embedded in a cement slab on alley No. 7, designated as No. 2010, "fragment display" on the Dead Space map and survey database

Interments in the Widow Paris tomb for which there are records in the Burial Books or Interment Payment Records, Office of Archives and Records:

5.

FAMILY, BABY (5)	COLORED	WP, NO VAULT (2)

François Glapion, colored, age 8 months, died May 18, 1834, son of Dominique [Christophe] Glapion and Marie Laveau.
Interred May 19, 1834
This early book gives no information on cause or place of death or description of the place of burial
Burial Book 1834-1835, p. 84
Funeral SLC May 18, 1834, vol. 10, part 3, p. 301, act 2019
No civil death certificate

6.

FAMILY, SLAVE	COLORED	WP, NO VAULT (3)
ADULT MALE		

Jean Louis, negro, age 69, slave of Marie Laveau Vve Paris, interred January 9, 1835.
Burial Book 1834-1835, p. 243

7.

FAMILY, ADULT MALE (6)	WHITE	WP, MIDDLE (4)

Christophe Duminy de Glapion (life partner of Marie Laveau)
There is no Burial Book for 1855. Register of St. Louis Cathedral Funeral Expenses for 1852-1855: *Enterrement de quatriesse classe de Christophe Dmy. de Glapion... Esposé rue Ste. Anne entre Bourgogne & Ramparts... enterrement cimre No. 1* (fourth class burial of Christophe Duminy de Glapion.... Viewing at St. Ann Street between Burgundy and Rampart... burial in cemetery No. 1). His name appears at the top of the middle tablet of the tomb as *Cphe Duminy De Glapion, décédé le 26 Juin 1855*

8.

FAMILY, ADULT FEMALE (7)	COLORED	WP, UPPER (1)

Madame Widow Oscar *née* Glapion, (possibly Eloise Glapion, daughter of Marie and Christophe) colored, native of Louisiana, age 34, died 152 St. Ann Street of consumption, Certificate of Dr. O. Anfour
Est decédée heir Rue Ste. Anne No. 252 de consomption Mme Vve Oscar née Glapion, native de la Louisiane, agée de 34 ans, inhumée dans la tombe de Mme Vve Paris née Laveau, trou de haut (died yesterday of tuberculosis, St. Anne Street No. 252 [152], Madame Widow Oscar, born Glapion, native of Louisiana aged 34 years)
Interred July 20,1860, in the tomb of Mme Vve Paris *née* Laveau, upper vault
Burial Book 1859-1864, p. 103
No civil death certificate

9.

FAMILY, CHILD (8)	COLORED	WP, NO VAULT (4)

Edouard Eastin (son of Pauline Gondron and Edouard Eastin, grand-nephew of Marie Laveau), colored, age 6 years, son of Edouard Easten and Louise [Pauline] Gendron died of diphtheria, certificate of Dr. Marmellon. Interred September 9, 1860, in the tomb of Mme Vve Paris
Burial Book 1859-1864, p. 48
No civil death certificate

10.

FAMILY, SLAVE	COLORED	WP, LOWER (1)
ADULT, FEMALE		

Marie, negresse slave of Mme Marie Laveau, died of old age, certificate of Dr. J. Labatut
Interred October 29, 1861, in the tomb of Marie Laveau Vve Paris, lower vault
Burial Book 1859-1864, p. 119
No civil death certificate

11.

BABY	COLORED	WP, MIDDLE (5)

Albert Young, colored, age 7 months, infant child of Josephine Cocher, died of diarrhea, certificate of Dr. Morrison, surgeon Charity Hospital
Interred June 5, 1863, in the tomb of Paris *née* Laveau, second aisle on the right, middle vault
Burial Book 1859-1864, p. 195
No civil death certificate

12.

BABY	COLORED	WP, NO VAULT (5)

Stillborn infant, colored, born at 249 St. Philip, certificate of Dr. Hy D'Aquin
Interred January 14,1865, in the tomb of Marie Laveau, third aisle [mistake?]
Burial Book 1859-1864, p. 97
No civil death certificate

13.

BABY	COLORED	WP, MIDDLE (6)

Henri Gaugnon, white, age 7 weeks, born corner of Villere and Carondolet Walk, died of variola [scarlet fever], certificate of Dr. D'Estouville
Interred March 1, 1865, in the Laveau tomb middle vault
Burial Book 1865-1869. p. 105
No civil death certificate

14.

BABY	COLORED	WP, NO VAULT (6)

William, colored, age 1 year 3 months, son of William Francis, died of dentition [teething] at 234 Mechanics between Villere and Robertson, certificate of Dr. W. Hy. Felise
Interred March 25, 1865, in the tomb of Marie Laveau.
Burial Book 1865-1869, p. 107
No civil death certificate

15.

BABY	COLORED	WP, NO VAULT (7)

Infant, issue of the Widow Paris [impossible], colored, died of phellama [?] at152 St. Ann, certificate of Dr. St. Romes
Interred October11, 1865, in the tomb of Veuve Paris.
Burial Book 1865-1869, p. 131
No civil death certificate

16.

FAMILY, BABY (9)	COLORED	WP, UPPER (2)

Eugènie Legendre, (daughter of Philomène   Glapion and Alexandre Legendre) colored, age 1 month, died of infant debility at 362 Grandhommes [now 1820 Dauphine, Faubourg Marigny], certificate of Dr. D'Aquin
Interred January 30,1866, in the upper vault of the tomb of Veuve Paris.
Burial Book 1865-1869, p. 146
Civil death certificate vol. 32, p. 225

17.

BABY	COLORED	WP, NO VAULT (8)

Eugene Legendre, (not child of Philomène and Alexandre) colored, age 5 hours, died July 31, 1866, at no 36 Craps [Burgundy, Faubourg Marigny], no cause of death given, certificate of Dr. Hy. D'Aquin.
Interred August 2, 1866, in the tomb of Veuve Paris *née* Laveau
Burial Book 1865-1869, p.168
No civil death certificate

18.

ADULT, FEMALE	COLORED	WP, PHEBE

Carmelite Feraud, colored, age 52, born St. James Parish, died of cholera, certificate of Dr. J Trudeau
Interred August 8, 1866, in the tomb of Marie Laveau inscribed *Phebé* on the slab.
Burial Book 1865-1869, p. 169
No civil death certificate

19.

ADULT, FEMALE	COLORED	WP, LOWER (2)

H. Muriolle Bejore, colored, age 33, died of asthma, certficate of Dr. L. Chaumette
Interred April 18, 1867, in the tomb of Marie Laveau lower vault
Burial Book 1865-1869, p. 107
No civil death certificate

20.

BABY	COLORED	WP, PHEBE

Felix Bertoulin, colored, age 13 months, died January 8 at No. 322 Claiborne of cholera, certificate of Dr. E.A. Murphy
Interred January 9, 1868, *dans la tombe de Marie Laveau par inscription Phebé* (in the tomb of Marie Laveau with the inscription Phebé)
Burial Book 1865-1869, p. 287
Civil death certificate vol. 36, p. 754

21.

ADULT, FEMALE	WHITE	WP, PHEBE

Madamoiselle Julie Traquet, white, age 24, native of Bugard Canton de Trie Hautes Pyrénées, France, died February 10 at 320 Orleans between Robertson and Claiborne of phithesis pulmonalis [tuburculosis], certificate of Dr. Castellanos
Interred February 11, 1869, in the tomb of *Phebé* owned by Marie Laveau *dit* Mme Paris between the first aisles on the left
Burial Book 1865-1869, p. 244
Civil death certificate vol. 44, p. 268

22.

BABY	WHITE	WP, LOWER (3)

Juliette Loubens, white, age 5 ½ months, died of *angeunce coisaneuse* [?] certificate of Dr. Alpuente

Interred March 12, 1869, in the lower vault of the tomb of Mme Veuve Paris, second aisle on the right

Burial Book 1865-1869, p. 357

Civil death certificate vol. 44, p. 824

23.

BABY	COLORED	WP, MIDDLE (7)

Antoine Cuney, black, age 1 year, died at 152 St. Ann Street [home of Marie Laveau] of cholera morbus, certificate of Dr. Wilson

Interred June 1, 1869, *dans la four du milieu de la tombe de Mme Paris dit Marie Laveau* (in the middle vault of the tomb of Mme Paris *dit* Marie Laveau)

Burial Book 1865-1869, p. 361

No civil death certificate

24.

FAMILY, BABY (10)	COLORED	WP, UPPER (3)

Joseph Legendre (son of Philomène Glapion and Alexandre Legendre), colored, age 1 month, died at 362 Dauphine [now 1820 Dauphine, Faubourg Marigny], no cause given, certificate of Dr. D'Aquin

Interred February 12, 1870, in the upper vault of the tomb bearing inscription Madame Paris *née* Laveau between the first and second aisles on the left

Burial Book 1870-1873, p. 111

Civil death certificate vol. 46, p. 897

25.

FAMILY, BABY (11)	COLORED	WP, UPPER (4)

Charles Legendre (son of Philomène Glapion and Alexandre Legendre, twin brother of Joseph), colored, age 5 months, died at 362 Dauphine [1820 Dauphine, Faubourg Marigny], no cause given, certificate of Dr. D'Aquin

Interred May 24, 1870, in the upper vault of the tomb bearing inscription Madame Paris *née* Laveau between the first and second aisles on the left.

Burial Book 1870-1873, p. 127

Civil death certificate vol. 47, p. 116

26.

ADULT, MALE	WHITE	WP, UPPER (5)
CLOSE NEIGHBOR		

Monsieur Dominique Moreau, white, age 67 years, native of Salies Haute Garonne, France, died of yellow fever at 192 Bourbon between St. Ann and Dumaine, certificate of Dr. Faget

Interred September 17, 1870, in the upper vault of the tomb of Mme Veuve Paris, second aisle

Burial Book 1870-1873, p. 151

Civil death certificate vol. 48, p. 530

27.

ADULT, MALE, NEIGHBOR	COLORED	WP, LOWER (3)

Etienne Felix, colored, age 40 years, born in this city, died October 11, 1870, of cancer at 360 Grandhommes [Dauphine, Faubourg Marigny, next to the Legendre home], certificate of Dr. D'Aquin.

Interred October 12,1870, in the lower vault of the tomb of Mme Veuve Paris *dit* Marie Laveau

Burial Book 1870-1873, p. 158

Civil death certificate vol. 48, p. 760

28.

FAMILY, ADULT, FEMALE (12)	COLORED	WP, UPPER (6)

A[delai] Aldina Crocker, (daughter of Eloise Glapion and Pierre Crocker) colored, age 26, *petit fille de Marie Laveau dit Mme Parisse* (granddaughter of Marie Laveau called Madame Paris), died September 9, 1871, of abscess of the lungs at 152 St. Ann, certificate of Dr. Cantrell

Interred September 10, 1871 in the upper vault, tomb of Famille Paris or Marie Laveau between first and second aisles to the left

Burial Book 1870-1873, p. 215

Civil death certificate vol. 52, p. 245, death reported by D. Gondron

29.

BABY	COLORED	WP, LOWER (5)

Caroline (Julien), colored, age 7 months, daughter of Charles Julien, died February 24, 1872, of bronchitis at 38 Craps [Burgundy in the Faubourg Marigny], certificate of Dr. D'Aquin

Interred February 25, 1872, *loué pour un an a la eaison de quinze piastres voute du bas sans marbre tombe propietaire Mme Paris* (Rented for one year for the consideration of fifteen dollars the lower vault without marble owned by Madame Paris). This is the first instance of the tomb being rented out.

Burial Book 1870-1873, p. 247

No civil death certificate

30.

ADULT, MALE, FRIEND	COLORED	WP, MIDDLE (8)

Mr Pierre Monette, colored, age 78 years, died April 24, 1872, of cerebral congestive fever at his home at 66 Casacalvo [466 Royal Street Faubourg Marigny], certificate of Dr. Gumbellet

Interred April 25, 1872, in the middle vault of the tomb of Mme Veuve Paris dit Marie Laveau, along with the remains of Madame Monette

Burial Book 1870-1873, p. 254

Civil death certificate vol. 54, p. 303, death reported by D. Gondron, 152 St. Ann

31.

BABY, FRIEND	COLORED	WP, UPPER (7)

Charles Albert Monette, colored, infant, born March 11, 1872, died of congestion of the brain at his parents' residence at 66 Casacalvo between Spain and Mandeville [Faubourg Marigny], certificate of Dr. Egland

Interred July12, 1872, in the upper vault of the Monette family tomb owned by Mme Veuve Paris between the first and second aisle on the left

Burial Book 1870-1873, p. 269

Civil death certificate vol. 55, p. 170. Death reported by J.J. Monette.

32.

FRIEND, ADULT, FEMALE	COLORED	WP, LOWER (6)

Mme Edouard Monette, colored, age 24 years, died August 11, 1872, of phithesis pulmonalis at No. 8 Poets Street [Washington, Faubourg Marigny], certificate of Dr. Ducatel
Interred August 12, 1872, in the lower vault of the tomb of Mme Veuve Paris second aisle on the right *sans marbre et avec couverture en blanche sans inscription* (without marble and with a white cover without inscription)
Burial Book 1870-1873, p. 274
Civil death certificate vol. 55, p. 359, death reported by Edouard Monette, 8 Poets Street

33.

ADULT, FEMALE	COLORED	WP, UPPER (8)

Miss Henriette Lameyer, colored, age 40 years, not married, mother born in Louisiana, father in Germany, died March 16, 1873, at 168 Erato of congestion of the brain, certificate of Dr. Roudanez
Interred March 17, 1873, in the upper vault of the tomb rented for one year with condition of renewal and transport of corpse to its proper place. This tomb situated in the 2nd aisle on right and is the property of Mme Veuve Paris *dit* Marie Laveau. [original in English]
Burial Book 1870-1873, p. 309
Civil death certificate vol. 57, p. 451

34.

BABY	WHITE?	WP, LOWER (7)

James Elgan, no race given [probably white], infant, died [stillborn?] at 383 Dumaine, home of Monsieur James Elgan, certificate of Dr. D'Aquin
Interred March 2, 1873, in the lower vault without marble tomb owned by Mme Veuve Paris second aisle on the right. Written over: transferred to the tomb of Lucien Brouchon [?] on the Conti Street aisle
Burial Book 1870-1873, p. 310
No civil death certificate

35.

BABY	WHITE	WP, LOWER (8)

Ida Durand, white, 14 months, died August 20, 1873, of meningitis at 229 St. Louis, certificate of Dr. Eslauris

Interred August 20, 1873, in the lower vault without marble of the tomb of Mme Veuve Paris second aisle on the right; rented for 12 months

Burial Book 1870-1873, p. 334

Civil death certificate vol. 59, p. 153, death reported by M. Durand, native of Maine, residing at 229 St. Louis Street

36.

FAMILY, BABY (13)	COLORED	WP, MIDDLE (9)

Henry Raphael Glapion, (possibly son of Alexis Célestin Glapion and Onesta Crocker, great-grandson of Marie and Christophe) colored, age 2 months, died of maramus infantus on September 14, 1873, at 152 St. Ann, certificate of Dr. Mosonnier

Interred September 15, 1873, in the middle vault, tomb of Mme Widow Paris between first and second aisle to left

Burial Book 1870-1873, p. 339

Civil death certificate vol. 59, p. 356, death reported by D. Gondron, 152 St. Ann

37.

CHILD,	WHITE	WP, UPPER (9)
CLOSE NEIGHBOR		

Corine Ayala, white, age 10 years, born in Havana, granddaughter of Joseph Ayala and Merida Serranos, died of tuberculosis on June 22, 1874, on Rampart between St. Ann and Dumaine, certificate Dr. Joasain DeGay

Interred June 22, 1874, in the upper vault of the *tombe sans marbre protriataire Mme Veuve Paris, 2me allée à droit* (tomb without marble owned by Madame Widow Paris second aisle on the right

Burial Book 1874-1881, p. 73

No civil death certificate

38.

FAMILY, BABY (14)	COLORED	WP, MIDDLE (9)

Antoine Raphael, (possibly son of Alexis Célestin Glapion and Onesta Crocker, great-grandson of Marie and Christophe) colored, age 1 month (newborn), died of general debility on October 17, 1874, "at his mother's residence 152 St. Ann Street between Burgundy and Rampart," certificate of Dr. John Dell Orto
Interred October 17, 1874, in the middle vault, *tombe de Mme Vve Paris dit Marie Laveau* (tomb of the Widow Paris called Marie Laveau)
Burial Book 1874-1881, p. 88
Civil death certificate vol. 62, p. 136, death reported by [Alexandre] Glapion Legendre of 152 St. Ann

39.

ADULT, FEMALE	WHITE	WP, MIDDLE (10)

Mme George Piene, white, age 50 years, died of apoplexy [stroke] on February 13, 1874, at 183 Ursulines, certificate Dr. Guinbelloh
Interred February 14, 1875, in the middle vault, *tombe appertenant à Mme Vve Paris seconde allée à droit* (tomb pertaining to Madame Widow Paris second aisle on the right)
Burial Book 1874-881, p. 103
No civil death certificate

40.

BABY	WHITE	WP, LOWER (9)

Joseph Paternos, white, age 1 year, died of *mort noyé* (drowning) on June 22, 1875, home address 154 Robertson, certificate of Coroner Fegue
Interred on June 22, 1875, in the lower vault of the tomb of Vve Paris
Burial Book 1874-1881, p. 124
No civil death certificate

41.

ADULT, FEMALE	WHITE	WP, UPPER (10)

Dame Vve François Mauberret [Clarisse Meilleur, widow of François Mauberret who died November 29, 1868], white, age 59 years, native of New Orleans, died on January 9, 1875, at her home at 254 St. Louis, of *ramollissement du cerveau* (softening of the brain), certificate of Dr. Dupaquer, homeopath
Interred January 10, 1875, in the upper vault of the tomb *portent inscription Marie Laveau*
Burial Book 1874-1881, p. 155
Civil death certificate vol. 65, p. 297

42.

CHILD	WHITE	WP, LOWER

Wilhemina Boucher, white, age 6 years (death certificate says 1 year, 4 months), native of New Orleans, died on February 29, 1876, of scarlet fever, at corner of Toulouse and Basin, certificate of Dr. Edw. Ackord
Interred March 1, 1876, in the tomb of Marie Laveau *façade en planche caveau du bas No. 1* (covered in planks lower vault No. 1) second aisle on the right
Burial Book 1874-1881, p. 162
Civil death certificate vol. 65, p. 599

43.

FRIEND, ADULT, MALE	WHITE	BIENVENU TOMB
		MOVED TO WP

Lucien Joseph Adams Jr., white, age 27, born in New Orleans, residence 400 Bienville, died April 6, 1876. of a gunshot wound, certificate of Dr. Chastant, coroner
Interred April 7, 1876, in the lower vault of the tomb portent inscription A.D. Bienvenu, allée du centre (bearing the inscription A.D. Bienvenu, center aisle). Written over: *le corps a été transferé dans la tombe a seconde allée a droite, tombe achétée de Philomene Laveau* (the body was transferred to the tomb second aisle on the right, tomb bought by [taken over by] Philomene Laveau
Burial Book 1874-1881, p. 168
No civil death certificate

44.

CHILD	COLORED	WP, LOWER (10)

Marie Aimée Evelot, colored, age 2 years, 3 months, died May 3, 1876, of measles on Dauphine Street, certificate of Dr. Bayou [possibly Jean Montaneé, known as Jean Bayou or Doctor John]
Interred May 3, 1876, in the lower vault of the tomb bearing inscription Famille Vve Paris, opening ordered by Vve Paris
Burial Book 1874-1881, p. 172
Civil death certificate vol. 66, p. 64

45.

FAMILY, BABY (15)	COLORED	WP, UPPER (11)

Manuel Legendre (possibly son of Philomène Legendre), colored, age 4 months, died May 9, 1876, at 152 St. Ann, of inflamation of the intestines, certificate of Dr. DellOrto
Interred May 10, 1876, in the upper vault of the tomb bearing inscription Famille Vve Paris, opening ordered by Mme Paris
Burial Book 1874-1881, p. 174
Civil death certificate vol. 66, p. 64, death reported by G. Wiltz, 210 Bourbon Street, who stated that "deceased was the lawful issue of Hermogene Legendre with Philomene Dauphine."

46.

ADULT, MALE	WHITE	WP, MIDDLE (11)

Lucien Gex, white, age 59 years, native of Savoie, France, died May 31, 1876, at 197 Tremé of *insuffisance avortegue*, certificate of Dr. D'Aquin.
Interred June 1, 1876, in the middle vault of the tomb *portant inscription Vve Paris*, second aisle from the left, opening ordered by *lauvin tombe loué* (renter of the tomb?). Written over: moved to St. Jacques, June 6, 1877
Burial Book 1874-1881, p. 180
Civil death certificate vol. 66, p. 338

47.

BABY	COLORED	WP, MIDDLE (12)

Justine, colored, age 11 months, native of New Orleans, died June 27, 1876, on Ursulines Street of cholera infantum, certificate of Dr. Gaudet
Interred June 27, 1876, in the middle vault of the tomb *portant inscription Vve Paris*, opening ordered by Vve Paris
Burial Book 1874-1881, p. 186
No civil death certificate

48.

BABY	WHITE	WP, UPPER (12)

Child of Joseph Berni, white, infant, died October 28, 1876, at 232 St. Ann Street of convulsions, certificate le Femme Sage Mme L. Vergez (midwife)
Interred October 29, 1876, in the upper vault of the tomb of Vve Paris, opening ordered by Joseph Berni
Burial Book 1874-1881, p. 207
No civil death certificate

49.

FAMILY, ADULT, FEMALE (16)	COLORED	WP, UPPER (13)

Celestine Glapion [Onesta Crocker] (daughter of Eloise Glapion and Pierre Crocker, granddaughter of Marie and Christophe), colored, age 23 years [born 1849, meaning she was actually 27], native of New Orleans, died November 22, 1876, at 152 St. Ann Street of phthisis pulmonalis [tuberculosis], certificate of Dr. Whendahl
Interred November 23, 1876, in the upper vault of the tomb bearing inscription Famille Vve Paris, opening ordered by Marie Laveau
Burial Book 1874-1881, p. 211
Civil death certificate vol. 67, p. 613, Célestin Glapion, residing on Aubry Street near Rocheblave Street in the city, declares that his wife Onesta Oscar Mansini, a native of New Orleans, aged twenty-two years, died on the twenty-second instant (Nov. 22nd 1876) at 152 St. Ann Street in this city

50.

ADULT, MALE	WHITE	WP, UPPER (14)
CLOSE NEIGHBOR		

John Eaton, white, age 63 years, native of Vermont, died January 5, 1877, on Rampart between St. Philip and Dumaine of a hemorrhage, certificate Dr. Faget
Interred January 6, 1877, in the upper vault of the tomb bearing inscription Vve Paris, opening ordered by Pierre Boyer, undertaker
Burial Book 1874-1881, p. 219
No civil death certificate

51.

BABY	WHITE	WP

Stillborn child of Mme Nicolas Perfenoff, white, born dead on rue de la Doune [Customhouse/Iberville], certificate of Dr. Moreau

Interred February 17, 1877, in the tomb bearing inscription Vve Paris situated in the second aisle on the right, *façade en planche* (front covered by planks), opening ordered by M. Couvain. [vault not specified]

Burial Book 1874-1881, p. 227

No civil death certificate

52.

ADULT, FEMALE	WHITE	WP, MIDDLE (13)

Jenny Forrest, white, age 40 years, native of Ireland, died September 21, 1877 of pernicious fever at 69 Rampart Street, certificate of Dr. Joseph Genos.

Interred September 22, 1877, in the center vault of the tomb bearing inscription Vve Paris

Burial Book 1874-1881, p. 257

Civil death certificate vol. 69, p. 870

53.

BABY	WHITE	WP, UPPER (15)

Felix Michel Gaudet, white, age 6 months, 21 days, born in New Orleans, residence corner St. Louis and Rampart, died February 2, 1878, of pneumonia, certificate of Dr. F.B. Gaudet.

Interred February 3, 1878, in the upper vault of the tomb bearing inscription Vve Paris; *loué ce jour* (rented this day) by Mr Chas U. Gaudet

Burial Book 1874-1881, p. 275

Civil death certificate vol. 71, p. 557

54.

BABY, CLOSE NEIGHBOR	COLORED	WP, LOWER (11)

Seliha or Leliha Fegue, colored, age 8 months, died April 19 of convulsions corner Burgundy and St. Ann, certificate of Dr. Castellanos

Interred April 20, 1878, in lower vault of the tomb bearing inscription Vve Paris, second aisle on the right, opening ordered by *sa fille Mlle Paris* (her daughter Miss Paris [Philomene Glapion Legendre])

Burial Book 1874-1881, p. 285

No civil death certificate

55.

BABY	COLORED	WP, LOWER (12)

Henry Gusman, white, age 8 months, born September 24, 1877, died May 30 of phthisis pulmonalis, certificate of Dr. F. de Roaldis

Interred May 31, 1878, in the lower vault of the tomb bearing inscription Vve Paris, rented by Manuel Cauvain, sexton St. Louis Cemetery No. 1. No notation that the body was moved.

Burial Book 1874-1881, p. 289

No civil death certificate

56.

BABY	COLORED	WP, LOWER (13)

Frank Johnson, colored, age 5 months, died August 9, 1878, of enteritis (food poisoning) at 263 St. Ann, certificate of Dr. Castellanos.

Interred August 9, 1878, in lower vault of the tomb bearing inscription Vve Paris, opening ordered by Mme Legendre)

Burial Book 1874-1881, p. 299

Civil death certificate vol. 71, p. 606

57.

BABY	WHITE	WP, LOWER (14)

L. Gueson, white, age 7 days, died August 31, 1878, at 225 Dauphine from tetanus, certificate of Sage Femme St. Bausset (midwife)

Interred September 1, 1878, in the lower vault of the tomb bearing inscription Famille Vve Paris, *façade en planche* (front covered by planks), second aisle on the right. Four interments of babies in lower vault within a year

Burial Book 1874-1881, p. 307

Civil death certificate vol. 71, p. 990

58.

CHILD	WHITE	ORIGINALLY IN LEGRAX
FAIRLY CLOSE NEIGHBOR		TOMB, MOVED TO WP,
		MOVED TO LOUISA STREET

Lucie Billard, white, age 4 years, died September 11, 1878, of yellow fever at the corner of Chartres and Bienville, certificate of Dr. Borde.
Interred September 12, 1878, in the tomb of Legrax. Written over: *le corps été transferé le 8 aout 1880 dans la tombe portent le nom Vve Paris. Transferé le 5 Avril 1881 a cimitiere Louisa* (the body was transferred on 8 August 1880 into the tomb bearing the name Widow Paris; transferred on 5 April 1881 to the Louisa Street Cemetery)
Burial Book 1874-1881, p. 317
No civil death certificate

59.

| CHILD | WHITE | WP, LOWER (15) |

Henry Bertrand, white, age 4 years, native of New Orleans, died September 11, 1878, of yellow fever at 246 Ursulines, certificate of Dr. L. Martin
Interred September 12, 1878, in the lower vault of the tomb bearing inscription Marie Lavau [*sic*] or Vve Paris, tomb *situe derriere allée du Crozat au gauche* (situated in the aisle behind the Crozat tomb on the left).
Opening ordered by Mme Legendre [Philomene Glapion Legendre]
Burial Book 1874-1881, p. 318
Civil death certificate vol. 73, p. 123

60.

| ADULT, FEMALE | WHITE | WP, MIDDLE (14) |

Angela Lapata (Sapata?), white, age 17 years, native of Mexico, died March 3, 1879, of phthisis at 218 Bourbon Street, certificate of H. Rancé, coroner
Interred March 4, 1879, in the middle vault of the tomb of the Family Widow Paris, rented by Cauvain. (in English)
Burial Book 1874-1881, p. 352
No civil death certificate

61.

BABY	COLORED	WP, LOWER (16)

Child of Josephine Tapoe, colored, age 7 months (later says stillborn), native of New Orleans, died May 4, 1880, at 265 Dumaine, certificate of H. Bezou, Coroner

Interred May 4, 1880, in the lower vault of the tomb bearing name Vve Paris, the tomb front frame planks, opening ordered by Philomene (in English)

Burial Book 1874-1881, p. 401

No civil death certificate

62.

ADULT, FEMALE, FRIEND	WHITE	WP, NO VAULT SPECIFIED

Widow Charles Fagot (Virginie Bienvenu, mother-in-law of Judge Lucien Adams), white, died of softening of the brain on May 6, 1881, at her residence at 400 Bienville, certificate of Dr. P. Tricou

Interred May 7, 1881, in the tomb of Bienvenu and Adams, center alley, opening by Adams' son. *Le corps èté transfere dans la tombeau achetée de Philomène Laveau seconde allée a droit* (the body was transferred to the tomb belonging to Philomène Laveau second aisle on the right)

Burial Book 1881-1883, p. 458

Civil death certificate vol. 78, p. 717

63.

FAMILY, ADULT, FEMALE (17)		
MARIE LAVEAU	COLORED	WP, MIDDLE (15)

Dame Christophe Glapion. Mrs. C. Glapion (Marie Laveau), colored, age 78 years, died of diarrhea on June 15, 1881, at her residence 152 St. Anne, certificate of Dr. J. DellOrto.

Interred June 16, 1881, in the middle vault of the family tomb of Vve Paris, opening ordered by Philomène Laveau.

Burial Book 1881-1883, p. 467

Civil death certificate vol. 78, p. 1113, death reported by A. Lamothe (Augustin Lamothe, listed in the 1880-81 city directory as a white bookkeeper residing at 152 St. Ann.)

64.

BABY	COLORED	WP, LOWER (17)

Joseph Fels, age 18 months, native of New Orleans, colored, died of diarrhea on November 21, 1881 at 224 Dumaine, certificate of Dr. Henry Bezou
Interred November 22, 1881, in the lower vault of the tomb of Vve Paris, opening ordered by Philomène
Burial Book 1881-1883, p. 491
Civil death certificate vol. 79, p. 949

65.

ADULT, MALE	WHITE	WP, LOWER (18)

Joseph Follin, white, age 14 years, native of Cuba, died April 11, 1883, at 46 St. Peter Street, of "general debility," certificate of Dr. Y.R. Lemonnier, coroner
Interred April 12, 1883, in the lower vault of the family tomb of Widow Paris or Marie Laveau, opening ordered by Philomene
Burial Book 1883-1886, p. 21
No civil death certificate

66.

CHILD	COLORED	WP, LOWER (19)

Delphine Llado, colored, age 3 years, 6 months, native of New Orleans, died of pneumonia on January 21, 1885, at 216 Dauphine Street, certificate of Dr. Barra
Interred January 22, 1885, in the lower vault of the family tomb of Marie Laveau, opening ordered by Philomene
Burial Book 1883-1886, p. 151
No civil death certificate

67.

ADULT, MALE, FRIEND	COLORED	WP, LOWER (20)

Charles Ernest Llado (probable brother of Ernestine Llado), colored, age 48, native of New Orleans, died of chronic tubercular laryngitis June 12, 1887, on Orleans near Galvez, certificate of Dr. Wiendahl
Interred June 13, 1887, in the family tomb of Vve Paris, lower vault, opening ordered by Philomène
Burial Book 1886-1892, p. 65
Civil death certificate vol. 91, p. 402

68.

CHILD, NEIGHBOR	COLORED	WP, UPPER (16)

Joseph Alexander McLean, colored, age 8, native of New Orleans, died of diphtheria February 28, 1889, at 81 St. Ann, certificate of Dr. E. Hincks

Interred March 1, 1889, in the family tomb of Vve Paris, upper vault, opening ordered by Philomène

Burial Book 1886-1892, p. 141

Civil death certificate vol. 94, p. 812

69.

ADULT, FEMALE	COLORED	WP, LOWER (21)

Pauline Vigne, colored, age 75, native of New Orleans, died of senile debility at 152 St. Ann Street on February 22, 1892, certificate of Dr. Parra

Interred February 24, 1892, in the family tomb of Wid. Paris lower vault, opening ordered by Mrs. Legendre

Burial Book 1886-1892, p. 274

Civil death certificate vol. 101, p. 329, death reported by A. Legendre [Alexandre Glapion Legendre] residing at 152 St. Ann Street

70.

ADULT, MALE, FAMILY (18)	COLORED	WP, UPPER (17)
	(IDENTIFIED AS WHITE)	

John Croker (Victor Pierre Crocker, son of Eloise Glapion and Pierre Crocker, grandson of Marie and Christophe) white, age 40, native of New Orleans, died of peritonitis (abdominal inflamation) at 219 Tremé on August 13, 1892, certificate of Dr. H.H. Parra

Interred August 14, 1892, in the Laveau family tomb upper vault, opening ordered by Mrs. Legendre

Burial Book 1886-1892, p. 300

Civil death certificate vol. 102, p. 551, death reported by his cousin, Alex Legendre. Although the record states that Crocker died at 219 Tremé, city directories show him and Alex Legendre living at 152 St. Ann.

71.

ADULT, MALE	COLORED	WP, LOWER (22)

Albert Becknou, age 34, colored, native of New Orleans, died of alcoholism at 1020 [formerly 152] St. Ann Street on September 5, 1894, certificate of Dr. Larra
Interred in Marie Laveau tomb lower vault, opening ordered by Philomène Legendre
Burial Book 1893-1900, p. 76
No civil death certificate

72.

CHILD, FAMILY (19)	COLORED	WP, UPPER (18)
	(IDENTIFIED AS WHITE)	

Antoinette Santenac (daughter of Noëmie Legendre and Benjamin Santenac, great-granddaughter of Marie and Christophe), age 10, white, native of New Orleans, died of drowning accident on September 16, 1894, home address 152 St. Ann, certificate of Dr. Maylie
Interred September 17, 1894, in family tomb of Marie Laveau upper vault, opening ordered by Glapion [Alexandre Glapion Legendre]
Burial Book 1893-1900, p. 77
No civil death certificate

73.

CHILD, FAMILY (20)	COLORED	WP, UPPER (19)
	(IDENTIFIED AS WHITE)	

Marita Santenac (daughter of Noëmie Legendre and Benjamin Santenac, great-granddaughter of Marie and Christophe), white, age 8, native of New Orleans, died of typhoid fever at 152 St. Ann Street on December 7, 1894, certificate of Dr. Parra
Interred December 8, 1894, in Marie Laveau family tomb upper vault, opening ordered by Glapion [Alexandre Glapion Legendre]
Burial Book 1893-1900, p. 85
Civil death certificate vol. 107, p. 575

74.

ADULT, FEMALE	COLORED	WP, NO VAULT SPECIFIED

Louise Johnson, age 35, colored, native of Louisiana, died of chronic tuberculosis at Charity Hospital on February 8, 1897, certificate of Dr. J.A. Leake

Interred February 8, 1897, in Philomène Glapion's little tomb, opening ordered by Emile [Labat?], undertaker

Burial Book 1893-1900, p. 175

75.

ADULT, FEMALE, FAMILY (21)	COLORED	WP, LOWER (23)

Ernestine Llado (domestic partner of Alexandre Glapion Legendre), age 32, died of phithisis pulmonalis at 1020 [formerly 152] St. Ann Street on March 26, 1897, certificate of Dr. Parra

Interred March 26, 1897, in family tomb of Philomène Glapion lower vault, opening ordered by Cordier, undertaker

Burial Book 1893-1900, p. 180

Civil death certificate vol. 113, p. 474

76.

BABY, FAMILY (22)	COLORED (IDENTIFIED AS WHITE)	WP, MIDDLE (16)

Clara Westenberg (daughter of Fidelia Legendre and Julius Westenberg, great-granddaughter of Marie and Christophe), age 4 months, white, native of St. Louis, Missouri, died of cholera infantome at 1020 [formerly 152] St. Ann Street on April 5, 1897, certificate of Dr. H. Parra

Interred April 5, 1897, in Madame Legendre family tomb middle vault, opening ordered by Noëmie Legendre

Burial Book 1893-1900, p. 181

Civil death certificate, vol. 113, p. 549; Clara's race was originally designated as "colored," crossed out and "white" written in

77.

CHILD, FAMILY (23)	COLORED	WP, MIDDLE (17)
	(IDENTIFIED AS WHITE)	

Mary Legendre (probably daughter of Ernestine Llado and Alexandre Glapion Legendre, great-granddaughter of Marie and Christophe), age 21 days, white, native of New Orleans, died of marasmis at 1020 [formerly 152] St. Ann Street on April 16, 1897, certificate of Dr. H. Parra
Interred April 16, 1897, in Madame Legendre tomb middle vault, no notation of opening.
Burial Book 1893-1900, p. 182
Civil death certificate vol. 113, p. 618

78.

ADULT, FEMALE, FAMILY (24)	COLORED	WP UPPER (20)

Philomène Legendre (daughter of Marie and Christophe), age 62, colored, died of bronchitis at 1020 St. Ann Street on June 11, 1897, certificate of Dr. A. Maestri
Interred June 11, 1897, in Veuve Paris family tomb, no notation of opening.
Burial Book 1893-1900, p. 189. "Marie Laveau's daughter" written in pencil in a different hand
Civil death certificate vol. 114, p. 15

79.

ADULT, MALE, FAMILY (25)	COLORED	WP, LOWER (24)

Alex Legendre (Alexandre Glapion Legendre, son of Philomène Glapion and Alexandre Legendre, grandson of Marie and Christophe), colored, age 43, native of New Orleans, died of abscess of lung at 1810 Columbus [between Prieur and Roman] on January 7, 1903, certificate of Dr. Borneo
Interred January 8, 1903, Laveau marie [sic] tomb lower vault, no notation of opening
Burial Book 1900-1912 book 1, p. 142
Civil death certificate vol. 128, p. 1184

80.

ADULT, FEMALE	COLORED	WP, LOWER (25)

Mrs. Camille Quintelle [Kintell], age 58, colored, native of New Orleans, died of cancer of mesentery at 2542 Columbus on March 9, 1904, certificate of Dr. Landry

Interred March 10, 1904, in Marie Laveau tomb lower vault, no notation of opening.

Burial Book 1900-1912 book 2, p. 188

Civil death certificate Camille Quintette, vol. 132, p. 173

81.

ADULT, MALE, FRIEND	COLORED	WP, LOWER (26)

Joseph Yado [Llado] (possible brother of Ernestine Llado), age 49 [?], colored, native of Louisiana, died of gastroenteritis at New Orleans [no street address] on April 7, 1910, certificate of Dr. Preterdon

Interred April 8, 1910, in Marie Laveau tomb lower vault opposite Monette, no notation of opening.

Burial Book 1900-1912 book 3, p. 406

No civil death certificate

82.

ADULT, FEMALE	COLORED	WP, LOWER (27)

Mrs. Mary Mathieu, age 48, colored, native of Louisiana, died of pulmonary tuberculosis at 1008 New Orleans on February 8, 1912, certificate of Dr. Romaguax (?)

Interred February 9, 1912, in Marie Laveau tomb, lower vault, no notation of opening.

Burial Book 1900-1912 book 3, p. 466

Civil death certificate vol. 154, p. 240

83.

ADULT, FEMALE	COLORED	WP, LOWER (28)

Julianne V. Philips, age 72, colored, native of New Orleans, died of influenza at 2308 Orleans on December 27, 1917, certificate of Dr. Rappannier.

Interred December 27, 1917, in Blair Legendre family tomb lower vault facing St. Louis Street back of Friedel tomb, opening ordered by Blair Legendre

Burial Book 1913-1919, p. 262

Civil death certificate vol. 170, p. 1088

84.

ADULT, FEMALE	BLACK	WP, LOWER (29)

Bertha Alcindor, age 69, no race given, native of New Orleans, died on August 15, 1957, Board of Health Permit #40108, Carr Llopis

Interred August 20, 1957, in Archange Glapion tomb, lot #9 (7) alley 2 left facing St. Louis Street (lower vault) folio #95. No notation of opening

Burial Book 1921-1973, p. 242

Civil death certificate City of New Orleans file no. 57 5620, death reported by Josephine Glapion

TOMB OWNED BY THE WIDOW PARIS
ST. LOUIS AISLE, ST. LOUIS CEMETERY NO. 1

RESEARCH IN THE BURIAL BOOKS AT THE
OFFICE OF ARCHIVES AND RECORDS
ARCHDIOCESE OF NEW ORLEANS

1.

ADULT, FEMALE	WHITE	ST. LOUIS

Odille Bedenke, white, age 17 years, born New Orleans, died of pneumonia, certificate of Dr. D'estouville.
Interred September 17, 1863, in the tomb of Marie Laveau, St. Louis aisle.
Burial Book 1859-1864, p. 204
No civil death certificate

2.

ADULT, FEMALE	COLORED	ST. LOUIS UPPER

Adele Chaperon, colored, age 20 years, no cause of death given, certificate of Dr. Borole.
Interred May16,1864, in the tomb of Marie Laveau, St. Louis aisle, upper vault, *pas de marbre* (no marble tablet)
Burial Book 1859-1864, p. 240
No civil death certificate

3.

BABY	NO RACE	ST. LOUIS UPPER

Elicia, no surname, no race, age 14 months, died on Frenchmen between Bons Infants and Morales, no cause of death, certificate of Dr. D'Aquin
Interred May 24, 1864, in the tomb of Marie Laveau, St. Louis aisle, upper vault
Burial Book 1859-1864, p. 242
No civil death certificate

4.

BABY	COLORED	ST. LOUIS

François Auguste, colored, age 3 months, died at 220 St. Peter of a "burning wound," certificate of Dr. D'estouville
Interred October 3, 1864, in the tomb of Vve Paris, St. Louis aisle
Burial Book 1859-1864, p. 273
Civil death certificate vol. 27, p. 145

5.

NO AGE	WHITE	ST. LOUIS

Victoria Constant, white, no age, of tracheitis [inflammation of the trachea] at 287 Orleans, certificate of Dr. Geiser
Interred September 7, 1865, in the tomb of Marie Laveau, St. Louis aisle
Burial Book 1865-1869, p. 127
No civil death certificate

6.

BABY	WHITE	ST. LOUIS

Gaston André Edouard D'Antry, white, age 17 months, born New Orleans, died of *permonie suite de bougole* [?] certificate of Dr. W. Weindahl
Interred March 4, 1869, in the tomb of Madame Veuve Paris, St. Louis aisle
Burial Book 1865-1869, p. 347
No civil death certificate

7.

BABY	WHITE	ST. LOUIS

Andrews [Anders?] Sabbgast, white, age 2 months, father from New England, mother from Ireland, died on September 19, 1873, of enteritis colite [colitis?] corner of St. Louis and Galvez, certificate of Dr. DeBlanc
Interred September 19, 1873 *dans la vielle tomb sur l'allée St. Louis tombe sans marbre proprietaire Veuve Paris* (In the old tomb without marble on the St. Louis aisle owner Widow Paris)
Burial Book 1870-1873, p. 339
No civil death certificate

8.

BABY	COLORED	ST. LOUIS

Gustave Buck, colored, age 6 months, born in Louisiana, died of accidental burning on January 24, 1874, at corner of Bagatelle and Craps [Pauger and Burgundy, Faubourg Marigny], certificate of John Grayer, coroner
Interred January 24, 1874, *dans la tombe sur l'allée St. Louis par Veuve Paris* (in the tomb of the Widow Paris on the St. Louis aisle)
Burial Book 1874-1881, p. 57
No civil death certificate

9.

BABY, NEIGHBOR	WHITE	ST. LOUIS

Wallace Boucher, white, age 1 year, died on March 9, 1876, of scarlet fever, at corner of Toulouse and Basin, certificate of Dr. Edw. Ackord

Interred March 10, 1876, in the tomb of Vve Paris *sur allée rue st. Louis pas de marbre* (on the St. Louis aisle without marble) [no vault]

Burial Book 1874-1881, p. 164

Civil death certificate vol. 65, p. 653

10.

ADULT, MALE, NEIGHBOR	BLACK	ST. LOUIS

Eugène Joseph Lajoie, black, age 24, native of New Orleans, died of organic disease of the heart on May 9, 1881, at 75 Orleans Street, certificate of Dr. H. Bezou

Interred May 10, 1881, in the Widow Paris tomb on St. Louis alley near the mortar bed, opening ordered by P. Laveau.

Burial Book 1881-1883, p. 458

Civil death certificate vol. 78, p. 743

11.

ADULT, FEMALE, NEIGHBOR	WHITE	ST. LOUIS

Fortuné Perrigore, white, age 44 years, died of apoplexy on June 22, 1883, at 144 St. Ann [corner of Burgundy], certificate of Dr. Y.R. Lemonnier, coroner

Interred June 22, 1883, in Marie Laveau's tomb situated on the St. Louis Street alley near the mortar bed, opening ordered by Philomene

Burial Book 1883-1886, p. 36

No civil death certificate

12.

ADULT, FEMALE, NEIGHBOR	COLORED	ST. LOUIS

Rosalie Barron, colored, age 50 years, native of Louisiana, died of phthisis pulmonalis on September 9, 1884, on Ursulines between Royal and Chartres, certificate of Dr. B. Barra

Interred September 19, 1883, in Marie Laveau's tomb near the mortar bed in middle of alley near Leopold Guichard's family tomb, opening ordered by Philomene

Burial Book 1883-1886, p. 128

No civil death certificate

13.

ADULT, FEMALE	WHITE	ST. LOUIS

Annie Forber, white, age 56 years, native of France, died of spinal meningitis
at Charity Hospital on February 28, 1886, certificate of Dr. H. Parra
Interred February 28, 1886 in Marie Laveau's old tomb near the mortar bed
near Jarraeu's tomb, opening ordered by Philomène Legendre
Burial Book 1886-1892, p. 3
No civil death certificate

Vault inscribed Lucy Henderson/Anderson, Basin Street Wall, Lower Range, No. 81

owned by the Widow Paris

Research in the Burial Books at the Office of Archives and Records Archdiocese of New Orleans

1.

ADULT, FEMALE	WHITE	WALL VAULT

Louisa, spouse of Augustin Peise, white, age 32 years, born in Genes, Italy, died of typhoid fever, certificate of P.T. Tricou
Interred December 5, 1865, in the *four* of Marie Laveau , inscription Lucy Henderson.
Burial Book 1865-1869, p. 136
No civil death certificate

2.

ADULT, MALE	COLORED	WALL VAULT

Papite Micou (male), colored, age 19 years, died March 11, 1876, of *noyé accidentellement* (accidental drowning) at Milneburgh on Lake Pontchartrain, certificate of Dr. LeBlanc, coroner
Interred March 12, 1876, *dans le four No. 81 portant inscription Lucy Anderson range du bas Vve Paris* (in thevault No. 81 bearing inscription Lucy Anderson, lower range Widow Paris)
Burial Book 1874-1881, p. 164
No civil death certificate

3.

ADULT, FEMALE	BLACK	WALL VAULT

Marie Louise Young, colored, age 19 years, native of St. Charles Parish, died December 12, 1882, of phthisis pulmonalis, at 90 South Basin Street, certificate of Dr. P. E. Archinard
Interred December 13, 1882, in the vault bearing name Lucy Anderson lower range facing Basin Street, opening ordered by Philomène
Burial Book 1881-1883, p. 558
No civil death certificate

4.

ADULT, FEMALE	COLORED	WALL VAULT

Demasthene Tapo, age 24, colored, died on May 9, 1884
Interred May 10, 1884, in the vault of Lucy Anderson, lower range backing
on Basin Street, opening ordered by Philomène
Burial Book 1883-1886, p. 99
Civil death certificate vol. 84, p. 1158

5.

ADULT, MALE	MEXICAN	WALL VAULT

Pradou Ouerto, age 75, Mexican, August 11, 1885
Interred August 11, 1885, in the family vault of Lucy Anderson lower range
backing on Basin Street, opening ordered by Philomène
Burial Book 1883-1886, p. 184
No civil death certificate

6.

BABY	UNKNOWN	WALL VAULT

Son of Antoine Edward and Maria Monte, no race specified, age 6 months,
died of marasmus on May 27, 1886, at St. Anthony between Bourbon and
Dauphine, certificate of Dr. J. F. Magonnier
Interred May 28, 1886, in the family vault of Lucy Anderson lower range
backing on "Bassin" Street, opening ordered by Philomène
Burial Book 1886-1892, p. 64
No civil death certificate

7.

BABY, NEIGHBOR	COLORED	WALL VAULT

Willie Martin, age 3 months, colored, native of New Orleans, died of
gastro enteritis at 130 Toulouse on November 2, 1888, certificate of Dr. E.J.
Moitose
Interred November 3, 1888, in the family vault of Lucy Anderson lower
range backing on "Bassin" Street, opening ordered by Philomène
Burial Book 1886-1892, p. 125
Civil death certificate vol. 94, p. 88

8.

ADULT, FEMALE	BLACK	WALL VAULT

Josephine Quinn, age 34, black, native of Louisiana, died of phithisis pulmonalis at Charity Hospital on June 25, 1889, certificate of Dr. Chas de Mahy
Interred June 26, 1889, in the family vault of Lucy Anderson lower range backing on "Bassin" Street, opening ordered by Philomène Laveau
Burial Book 1886-1892, p. 156
No civil death certificate

9.

ADULT, FEMALE, NEIGHBOR	COLORED	WALL VAULT

Mrs. Allan Smith, age 60, colored, native of New Orleans, died of gastro hepititis at 140 Toulouse on June 27, 1890, certificate of Dr. E.J. Moiton.
Interred June 27, 1890, in the family vault of Lucy Anderson lower range backing on "Bassin" Street, opening ordered by Philomène Laveau
Burial Book 1886-1892, p. 198
Civil death certificate vol. 97, p. 500

10.

ADULT MALE, NEIGHBOR	UNKNOWN	WALL VAULT

Antonio Jaffa, age 24, died of pulmonary tuberculosis at 64 St. Philip Street on August 23, 1895, certificate of Dr. Theard
Interred August 23, 1895, in the family vault of Lucy Enderson [Anderson] lower range backing on "Bassin" Street, opening ordered by Philomène.
Burial Book 1893-1900, p. 120
No civil death certificate

11.

ADULT, FEMALE	COLORED	WALL VAULT
(FORMER NEAR NEIGHBOR?)		

Louise Baptist, age 58, native of New Orleans, died of chronic entestenstiles nephritis at 1010 St. Ann on January 26, 1901, certificate of Dr. S.S. Moiton
Interred January 26, 1901, "barried" in Philomene Glapion vault "baquin" on Basin Street, opening ordered by Blair Legendre
Burial Book 1900-1912, part 1 , p. 69
Civil death certificate vol. 124, p. 170

12.

ADULT, MALE	COLORED	WALL VAULT

Gustave Anderson, age 32, colored, native of New Orleans, died of tuberculosis at 2024 Orleans on July 17, 1903, certificate of Dr. Rappannier
Interred July 17, 1903, in the vault of Lucy Anderson lower range backing on "Bassin," no notation of opening or undertaker
Burial Book 1900-1912, part 1, p. 162
Civil death certificate vol. 130, p. 422

13.

ADULT, MALE	COLORED	WALL VAULT

George Capla, age 32, colored, native of Louisiana, died of tuberculosis in New Orleans [no street address] no date given [between December 16 and 18, 1910], no certifying doctor.
Interred [no date, 1910, in Lucy Anderson vault lower range backing on "Bassin," no notation of opening or undertaker
Burial Book 1900-1912, part 3, p. 428
Civil death certificate vol. 151, p. 18 (December 17)

Made in United States
Orlando, FL
24 September 2023

37245721R00065